OPPOSING VIEWPOINTS® SERIES

The Future of Higher Education

Other Books of Related Interest

Opposing Viewpoints Series
Banned Books
The Corporatization of America
Educational Equity

At Issue Series
Athlete Activism
Mob Rule or the Wisdom of the Crowd?
Student Debt

Current Controversies Series
The Business of College Sports: Who Earns What
Freedom of Speech on Campus
Historical Revisionism

> "Congress shall make no law … abridging the freedom of speech, or of the press."
>
> *First Amendment to the U.S. Constitution*

The basic foundation of our democracy is the First Amendment guarantee of freedom of expression. The Opposing Viewpoints series is dedicated to the concept of this basic freedom and the idea that it is more important to practice it than to enshrine it.

The Future of Higher Education

Sharmila Pixy Ferris and
Kathleen Waldron, Book Editors

Published in 2024 by Greenhaven Publishing, LLC
2544 Clinton Street,
Buffalo NY 14224

Copyright © 2024 by Greenhaven Publishing, LLC

First Edition

All rights reserved. No part of this book may be reproduced in any form without permission in writing from the publisher, except by a reviewer.

Articles in Greenhaven Publishing anthologies are often edited for length to meet page requirements. In addition, original titles of these works are changed to clearly present the main thesis and to explicitly indicate the author's opinion. Every effort is made to ensure that Greenhaven Publishing accurately reflects the original intent of the authors. Every effort has been made to trace the owners of the copyrighted material.

Cover image: Shutter z/Shutterstock.com

Library of Congress CataloginginPublication Data
 Names: Ferris, Sharmila Pixy, editor. | Waldron, Kathleen, editor.
Title: The future of higher education / edited by Sharmila Pixy Ferris and Kathleen Waldron.
Description: First edition. | New York : Greenhaven Publishing, 2024. | Series: Opposing viewpoints | Includes bibliographical references and index.
Identifiers: ISBN 9781534509412 (pbk.) | ISBN 9781534509429 (library bound)
Subjects: LCSH: Education, Higher--United States--Evaluation. | Education, Higher--Aims and objectives--United States. | Education, Higher--Social aspects--United States. | Education, Higher--Political aspects--United States.
Classification: LCC LA227.4 F888 2024 | DDC 378.73--dc23

Manufactured in the United States of America

Website: http://greenhavenpublishing.com

Contents

The Importance of Opposing Viewpoints	11
Introduction	14

Chapter 1: What Is the Value of Higher Education in the United States?

Chapter Preface	21
1. The Value of a College Education *Pew Research Center*	23
2. Reasons Not to Go to College *Imed Bouchrika*	33
3. The Effect of Student Debt on the Economy *Peter G. Peterson Foundation*	43
4. Removing Financial Barriers to Higher Education and Career Success *Timothy A. Poynton, Richard T. Lapan, and Amanda M. Marcotte*	48
Periodical and Internet Sources Bibliography	59

Chapter 2: Are There Suitable Alternatives to Traditional Higher Education?

Chapter Preface	62
1. The Benefits of Community College *Eileen Hoenigman Meyer*	64
2. Factors Contributing to Low Success Rates for Community College Students *Amy Hankins and Christine Harrington*	70
3. Can Stackable Credentials Offer an Alternative to a College Degree? *Robert A. Scott*	80

4. Are Online Learning and For-Profit Colleges the
   Future of Higher Education? **85**
   Gary E. McCullough and Andrew Hibel

Periodical and Internet Sources Bibliography **96**

Chapter 3: Can Higher Education Help Address Social Issues?

Chapter Preface **99**

1. Do the Humanities Make Students Better Employees
   and Citizens? **101**
   Kevin Reilly, Charles Steger, James Barker, and J. Bernard Machen

2. How the Debate on Diversity and Equity Came to
   Dominate Education **107**
   Matt Grossman, Carson Byrd, and Jonathan Collins

3. Valuing the Civic Role of University Education **118**
   Pedro Nuno Teixeira and Manja Klemenčič

4. Why Diversity, Equity, and Inclusion Programs
   Benefit Colleges **129**
   Erica Jacqueline Licht

Periodical and Internet Sources Bibliography **133**

Chapter 4: What Rights Are Protected in Higher Education?

Chapter Preface **135**

1. A Student Should Have the Privilege of Just Being
   a Student **137**
   ACUI

2. Four Fundamental Principles for Upholding
   Freedom of Speech on Campus **143**
   Adrienne Stone

3. Academic Freedom as a Source of Rights' Violations **150**
   Monika Stachowiak-Kudla

4. Academic Research Funded by Big Companies Is
    Compromised   **157**
    Lisa Bero
Periodical and Internet Sources Bibliography   **163**

For Further Discussion   **165**
Organizations to Contact   **167**
Bibliography of Books   **171**
Index   **173**

The Importance of Opposing Viewpoints

Perhaps every generation experiences a period in time in which the populace seems especially polarized, starkly divided on the important issues of the day and gravitating toward the far ends of the political spectrum and away from a consensus-facilitating middle ground. The world that today's students are growing up in and that they will soon enter into as active and engaged citizens is deeply fragmented in just this way. Issues relating to terrorism, immigration, women's rights, minority rights, race relations, health care, taxation, wealth and poverty, the environment, policing, military intervention, the proper role of government—in some ways, perennial issues that are freshly and uniquely urgent and vital with each new generation—are currently roiling the world.

If we are to foster a knowledgeable, responsible, active, and engaged citizenry among today's youth, we must provide them with the intellectual, interpretive, and critical-thinking tools and experience necessary to make sense of the world around them and of the all-important debates and arguments that inform it. After all, the outcome of these debates will in large measure determine the future course, prospects, and outcomes of the world and its peoples, particularly its youth. If they are to become successful members of society and productive and informed citizens, students need to learn how to evaluate the strengths and weaknesses of someone else's arguments, how to sift fact from opinion and fallacy, and how to test the relative merits and validity of their own opinions against the known facts and the best possible available information. The landmark series Opposing Viewpoints has been providing students with just such critical-thinking skills and exposure to the debates surrounding society's most urgent contemporary issues for many years, and it continues to serve this essential role with undiminished commitment, care, and rigor.

The key to the series' success in achieving its goal of sharpening students' critical-thinking and analytic skills resides in its title—Opposing Viewpoints. In every intriguing, compelling, and engaging volume of this series, readers are presented with the widest possible spectrum of distinct viewpoints, expert opinions, and informed argumentation and commentary, supplied by some of today's leading academics, thinkers, analysts, politicians, policy makers, economists, activists, change agents, and advocates. Every opinion and argument anthologized here is presented objectively and accorded respect. There is no editorializing in any introductory text or in the arrangement and order of the pieces. No piece is included as a "straw man," an easy ideological target for cheap point-scoring. As wide and inclusive a range of viewpoints as possible is offered, with no privileging of one particular political ideology or cultural perspective over another. It is left to each individual reader to evaluate the relative merits of each argument—as he or she sees it, and with the use of ever-growing critical-thinking skills—and grapple with his or her own assumptions, beliefs, and perspectives to determine how convincing or successful any given argument is and how the reader's own stance on the issue may be modified or altered in response to it.

This process is facilitated and supported by volume, chapter, and selection introductions that provide readers with the essential context they need to begin engaging with the spotlighted issues, with the debates surrounding them, and with their own perhaps shifting or nascent opinions on them. In addition, guided reading and discussion questions encourage readers to determine the authors' point of view and purpose, interrogate and analyze the various arguments and their rhetoric and structure, evaluate the arguments' strengths and weaknesses, test their claims against available facts and evidence, judge the validity of the reasoning, and bring into clearer, sharper focus the reader's own beliefs and conclusions and how they may differ from or align with those in the collection or those of their classmates.

Research has shown that reading comprehension skills improve dramatically when students are provided with compelling, intriguing, and relevant "discussable" texts. The subject matter of these collections could not be more compelling, intriguing, or urgently relevant to today's students and the world they are poised to inherit. The anthologized articles and the reading and discussion questions that are included with them also provide the basis for stimulating, lively, and passionate classroom debates. Students who are compelled to anticipate objections to their own argument and identify the flaws in those of an opponent read more carefully, think more critically, and steep themselves in relevant context, facts, and information more thoroughly. In short, using discussable text of the kind provided by every single volume in the Opposing Viewpoints series encourages close reading, facilitates reading comprehension, fosters research, strengthens critical thinking, and greatly enlivens and energizes classroom discussion and participation. The entire learning process is deepened, extended, and strengthened.

For all of these reasons, Opposing Viewpoints continues to be exactly the right resource at exactly the right time—when we most need to provide readers with the critical-thinking tools and skills that will not only serve them well in school but also in their careers and their daily lives as decision-making family members, community members, and citizens. This series encourages respectful engagement with and analysis of opposing viewpoints and fosters a resulting increase in the strength and rigor of one's own opinions and stances. As such, it helps make readers "future ready," and that readiness will pay rich dividends for the readers themselves, for the citizenry, for our society, and for the world at large.

Introduction

> "[The University] is the rare place in our society where there is a willingness to entertain odd ideas, even those profoundly outside mainstream discourse today, and where people find synergies and sympathies across time, space, and ideology that they did not think could exist."
>
> -Matthew Hartley, deputy dean, professor of education, and Board of Advisors Chair of Education at the University of Pennsylvania

In recent years, events across the United States related to higher education have proliferated, regularly hitting the headlines throughout the media channels in the country. Raucous debates about student debt, academic freedom, free speech in the classroom, faculty rights, student activism, college governance, presidential responsibility, library reading lists, curricula content, and the role of parents all surfaced among the body politic, often fueled by politicians seeking issues that would resonate with voters. Almost daily, there appears an article claiming that a college degree is no longer worth it from a financial point of view, stating that the cost of education does not yield a return on investment in the form of a career that compensates for the costly expense of college. The counter argument quickly appears, positing that college is not just about getting a high paying job but encompasses personal growth, life skills, critical thinking, and good citizenship. Student loan debt is too high, some argued while the federal government considered a debt forgiveness plan, and some states actually enacted local relief. Students held their breath in 2023, hoping some relief would be forthcoming.

The decline in undergraduate enrollment in the past two decades is a noticeable trend with far reaching implications. In 2010, there were approximately 22 million people attending either full or part-time colleges or universities in the country. By 2021, that number had dropped by 12 percent to 19 million and is likely to continue to decline over the next decade.[1] Why enrollments are declining is a point of debate. On the one hand, it is often attributed to the high cost of education, which prevents many individuals from aspiring to a college degree. On the other hand, that explanation, while true, ignores the overall demographics of the country and the effect of economic cycles on college enrollments. One must study overall population data to fully understand the dynamic. There are fewer students in high school today than there were ten years ago because a smaller percentage of the population of the country is at the age when traditional students attend high school. Therefore, there are fewer high school graduates preparing to go to college upon graduation than in the past. Of course, this demographic trend varies by state and region, but in general, it holds true.

In addition, economic cycles have a significant effect on whether or not people pursue an advanced degree, especially for men. When the economy is strong and jobs are plentiful, many people do not see the necessity for higher education and enter the workforce instead. When the economy enters a recession and jobs are scarce, the opposite can occur where people will begin or return to college, often as adults, because they believe additional educational credentials will help them enter and remain in the workforce. The very nature of work has changed with the rise of new technical skilled jobs not necessarily tied to traditional degree programs. Alternative providers of degrees, education, and credentials have proliferated so that student choice is much broader than it has ever been. Students have more choices than they did a few years ago. One can pursue a traditional four-year degree or earn a two-year degree and then transfer to a four-year institution. Or one can enroll in skill-specific online or in-person courses to earn a credential recognized in the marketplace as an entry point for certain jobs, in effect bypassing regular institutions of higher education. The variety of programs offered can be overwhelming to many people who might not fully grasp the differences within the educational landscape in the country today. In addition, gaining ongoing credentials in a transforming job market now appears to be a path many will face over the next few decades of a career, again a somewhat newer model of professional advancement.

The cost of higher education is a major discussion in the country today. Some economists point to the significant rise in tuition at most institutions over the past 20 years, whether public or private, noting that the investment required to complete a degree requires students to take on significant debt [2,3]. In addition, some posit that the required investment is not worth it as measured by post-graduate salaries and lifetime earnings. The economics of the cost of education and student debt are quite complex. Comparisons between public institutions and private institutions confuse an easy understanding of true cost as does the listed tuition price, which is very rarely the true cost of attendance. To complicate cost further, the availability of government and private sector loans, scholarships, and subsidized tuitions make the estimation of total cost to be very complicated if not misleading in many instances. Today, an undergraduate student who completes a four-year degree has an average debt of $28,950 upon graduation[4,5], mostly owed to the federal government. Most economists will argue that this level of debt should not be too burdensome over the course of a working life, while others argue that the individual debt level will delay purchasing a home, starting a family, and saving for the future. The reasons for the rise in tuition over the past decade or more are not fully understood, and critics will often blame administrators for poor management and wasteful spending. For public institutions, the proportional decline in state funding of higher education over the years is often overlooked as a contributing factor to higher tuition. Each state is different, with some states recently admitting to underfunding and taking steps to correct the situation while other states cannot do so either for financial reasons or for political reasons.

Despite the issue of cost, if one accepts that post-secondary education is worthwhile and vital for economic well-being and a good life—and not everyone holds this belief—then what type of education should be obtained? In 2020, the COVID-19 pandemic transformed many institutions of higher education, which suddenly shut their residence halls and sent students home in the middle of the spring term, ceasing to offer in-person classroom education and introducing emergency online courses. After three years, it is clear that higher education has been deeply affected by the transformation of pedagogy, and the long-term results of this transition have yet to be determined. Nevertheless, more students are taking fully online courses than they did only a few years ago, and this has opened the door to non-traditional educational institutions to provide alternative credentials, courses, and degrees to the country and world. The transition has contributed to the belief that a traditional college degree may not be as worthwhile as it once was or that a residential experience may not be necessary.

The role of higher education in addressing social issues in the United States is an additional point of debate that has seen an increased intensity of late. This has always been a point of discussion in the country and within the academy. Throughout the history of the country, scholars can point to moments when the most pressing national social issues engulfed the discourse on campuses. Learned centers with highly educated faculty who are experts in their fields are natural environments for proffering new ideas in society or challenging long-held beliefs. Controversy is created, the independence of the university is questioned, some faculty are removed from their positions because of their views, students protest, and authorities threaten to close down the enterprise. While perhaps natural and historic, it is still disconcerting for each generation, especially young people, to feel threatened for their beliefs. Developing rules of conduct while preventing intolerance is a major challenge for institutions of higher education, which are attempting to deal with society's most controversial issues. It is an exciting time on campus, but also a very challenging one.

Opposing Viewpoints: The Future of Higher Education is structured around four broad topics. Chapter 1 is about the purpose and value of higher education. Chapter 2 is about the different options students have for obtaining higher education degrees and/or credentials in the United States. Chapter 3 concerns the role of higher education and its institutions in addressing major social issues facing the nation. Chapter 4 addresses the role of student activism, issues of free speech on campus, and the intellectual property rights of institutions, students, and professors. Each chapter is divided into relevant and connected subtopics, with viewpoints by experts expressing different perspectives.

While we have addressed opposing viewpoints on several key trends in higher education, we ask that the reader keep in mind that the viewpoints addressed here are dynamic and can change rapidly in response to various factors including (ongoing) societal, economic, political, and technological shifts. Nevertheless, we hope the selection of viewpoints provides diverse perspectives and intriguing arguments for our readers.

References

1. National Center for Education Statistics, "Undergraduate Enrollment," U.S. Department of Education, Institute of Education Sciences, 2022. https://nces.ed.gov/programs/coe/indicator/cha.
2. Tracy Scott, "Is A College Education Worth The Student Loan Debt?" Northeastern University, n.d. https://bachelors-completion.northeastern.edu/news/is-a-degree-worth-student-loan-debt/
3. Timothy A. Poynton, Richard T. Lapan, Amanda M. Marcotte. "Financial Planning Strategies Of High School Seniors: Removing Barriers To Career Success." *The Career Development Quarterly*, 63, (1), pp. 57–73, 2015. https://doi.org/10.1002/j.2161-0045.2015.00095.x.

4. National Center for Education Statistics, "Price Of Attending An Undergraduate Institution," *Conditions of Education*. U.S. Department of Education, Institute of Education Sciences, 2023. https://nces.ed.gov/programs/coe/indicator/cue.
5. National Center for Education Statistics, "Loans For Undergraduate Students," *Conditions of Education*, U.S. Department of Education, Institute of Education Sciences, 2023. https://nces.ed.gov/programs/coe/indicator.cub.

CHAPTER 1

What Is the Value of Higher Education in the United States?

Chapter Preface

The nature and scope of U.S. colleges and universities have shifted over the last two centuries in response to changing society, politics, economics, and demographics[1], with changes dramatically accelerating as the 21st century approached. In the 19th century, higher education was quite exclusive, limited mostly to men and to the economically and socially privileged. The 20th century saw the increasing democratization of higher education, augmented by the rise of the middle class and the GI Bill, which provided educational funding to many soldiers returning from World War II. By the end of the 20th century, education was theoretically available to all, with increasing access to women, minorities, and people with fewer economic resources. However, many barriers to accessing higher education still existed as costs rose and student debt ballooned, exacerbated by the effects of the COVID-19 pandemic and the closing of traditional campuses for many months. Technological developments offered opportunities but also created barriers with digital divides created along socio-economic lines.

Historically in the United States, higher education was largely perceived as valuable, with clear economic benefits accruing over the lifetime for students completing degrees. This value, however, has come into sharp question in the 21st century as tuition costs rise sharply, student debt burgeons, and public scrutiny of colleges and universities increases. The costs of a college degree have risen over the years to the point that many cannot afford college today, while, relatedly, low income and minority students who do go to college often face systemic barriers to success.

The issue of student debt has been a point of political contention in Washington, DC. In August 2022, the administration of President Joe Biden spread the word of a plan to forgive $10,000 to $20,000 in student loan debt for millions of borrowers. The plan faced legal challenges, however, and the Supreme Court ultimately ruled it unconstitutional in July 2023. Financial challenges are reflected in falling enrollments as more high school graduates choose not to go to college.

Higher education's adaptability to changing times has never been tested more strongly than today, with the effects of the COVID-19 pandemic of 2020 still in play, as the pandemic exacerbated many of the underlying challenges faced by colleges and universities in the U.S. and globally).[2]

This chapter addresses themes of importance to higher education today including changed perceptions of the value of higher education and return on investment (ROI); barriers to higher education such as rising costs, student debt, and systemic barriers faced by lower income students; the evolving purpose of higher education, away from a focus on intellectual and personal growth to a focus on workforce preparation; and a focus on diversity and inclusivity, for all students to gain an equally valuable college experience. The viewpoints in this chapter not only present opposing perspectives on these themes but also offer practical advice that can assist those considering the purpose and value of higher education.

References

1. Hilary Wilder and Sharmila Pixy Ferris, "Communication Technology and the Evolution Of Knowledge," *The Journal of Electronic Publishing, 9(2)*, 2006. DOI: https://doi.org/10.3998/3336451.0009.201
2. Sharmila Pixy Ferris and Kathleen Waldron. *Thriving In Academic Leadership*, in press. Bingley, UK: Emerald Publishing.

VIEWPOINT 1

> "A majority of Americans (58%) say that workforce-relevant skills and knowledge are more important than personal and intellectual growth when it comes to the purpose of college."

The Value of a College Education

Pew Research Center

This viewpoint by the Pew Research Center reports on Americans' attitudes towards the purpose of higher education. Americans view workforce-relevant skills and knowledge as more important than personal and intellectual growth. Citing a survey that found that just 16 percent of Americans think that a four-year degree prepares students very well for a well-paying job in today's economy, the authors suggest that many Americans believe that the primary purpose of college is to prepare students for the workforce, rather than to help them grow personally and intellectually. Americans' opinions on the purpose of higher education seem to be divided along political lines and age. The Pew Research Center is an American think tank that provides information on social issues, public opinion, and demographics.

"The value of a college education," Pew Research Center, October 6, 2016.

As you read, consider the following questions:

1. What are the main arguments for the value of a college education presented in this viewpoint?
2. What factors contributed to the shift in public opinion regarding the purpose of college?
3. What is the "credentials gap" discussed in the viewpoint?

An extensive body of research has argued that obtaining a college diploma is a good deal for graduates on almost any measure—from higher earnings to lower unemployment rates. By the same token, those without a college degree can find their upward mobility in the job market limited by a lack of educational credentials: This survey finds that one-third of Americans who lack a four-year college degree report that they have declined to apply for a job they felt they were qualified for, because that job required a bachelor's degree.

But despite the potential benefits and opportunities available to college graduates—and the potential challenges faced by those who lack a college diploma—Americans have somewhat mixed attitudes about the effectiveness of traditional four-year colleges and other higher education institutions. On a personal level, many college graduates describe their own educational experience as having a generally positive impact on their personal and professional development. Roughly six-in-ten (62%) college graduates with two- or four-year degrees think their degree was very useful for helping them grow personally and intellectually, while roughly half think it was very useful for opening up job opportunities (53%) or for providing them with useful job-related skills and knowledge (49%).

Yet even as many college graduates view their own educational experience in positive terms, the public as a whole—including a substantial share of college graduates—expresses reservations about the extent to which various higher education institutions prepare students for the workforce more generally. Just 16% of

Americans think that a four-year degree prepares students very well for a well-paying job in today's economy, and 51% say this type of degree prepares students "somewhat well" for the workplace. Some 12% think that a two-year associate degree prepares students very well (46% say somewhat well), and 26% feel that certification programs in a professional, technical, or vocational field prepare students very well (52% say somewhat well).

The Purpose of College: Americans View Workforce-Relevant Skills and Knowledge as More Important than Personal and Intellectual Growth

Americans' views of what a college education should be tend to prioritize specific, workplace-related skills and knowledge rather than general intellectual development and personal growth. Half of Americans say that the main purpose of college should be to teach specific skills and knowledge that can be used in the workplace, while 35% think its main purpose should be to help students grow and develop personally and intellectually and 13% volunteer that these objectives are equally important. The public's views on this issue have shifted slightly in favor of skills development since the last time Pew Research Center asked this question in 2011. At that point, 47% said the main purpose of college should be to teach specific skills and knowledge and 39% said it should be to promote personal and intellectual growth.

Americans who have engaged in additional schooling beyond a bachelor's degree are especially likely to say that the main purpose of college should be personal and intellectual growth, rather than the acquisition of specific skills and knowledge. Some 47% of those with a postgraduate or professional degree think the main purpose of college should be personal and intellectual growth, while 35% think it should be teaching workplace-relevant skills.

In contrast, those with limited college experience (or no college experience at all) are more likely to prioritize the development of specific skills over general intellectual improvement. For instance, 56% of Americans with a high school diploma or less say college should be primarily a place to develop specific work-oriented knowledge and skills, while just 31% see it primarily as a place for personal and intellectual growth.

There is also a partisan element to these views, with Republicans and Democrats expressing highly differing opinions on the purpose of college. Democrats (including Democratic-leaning independents) are about evenly split on which of these objectives is more important: 42% say colleges should prioritize personal and intellectual growth, while 43% say they should prioritize the development of workforce-relevant skills. But among Republicans and Republican leaners, 58% say that the

THE COST OF HIGHER EDUCATION

The cost of college, including the expense of living and the cost of tuition and course materials, is the biggest barrier to post-secondary education for students.

Not surprisingly, current, future and students who dropped out say "free college" would have the single biggest impact on them finishing or returning to post-secondary education, according to the *Barriers to Post-Secondary Education Report* from Cengage Group, a global education technology company.

The company surveyed more than 1,600 current college students, recent high school graduates and students who have dropped out of post-secondary education to better understand their education barriers and what would have the biggest impact on them completing their education.

"Access to quality post-secondary education, be it in the form of a traditional degree or a skills-based certification, provides a clear path to job opportunities and economic mobility, however students need more affordable and flexible options," said Michael Hansen, CEO of Cengage.

Findings include:

- **Students go to college to get a job.** The number one reason current and potential students enroll/would enroll in college is because they say it is necessary for their career path and job opportunities after school (48 percent). Four-year college main purpose of college should be to teach specific skills—while just 28% feel that the main purpose should be general personal and intellectual growth.

These partisan differences hold true even after accounting for differences in educational attainment. Democrats and Democratic leaners with high levels of educational attainment are more likely to prioritize personal and intellectual growth relative to Democrats and Democratic leaners with lower levels of educational attainment.

But Democrats and Democratic-leaning independents at all educational levels are more likely than Republicans and Republican-

> students are more likely to say they enrolled to expand their social and/or professional networks than students at two-year or technical colleges.
> - **Cost is the biggest education barrier for current, future and former students.** High school graduates are more concerned with cost of tuition and course materials while current students and former students (those who have dropped out) are more concerned with the cost of living.
> - **"Free college" would have the biggest impact on students finishing or returning to post-secondary education.** Nearly half (46 percent) of students and adults said "free college" would have the greatest impact on them finishing or returning to school. Respondents who had dropped out were more likely to state past student debt forgiveness as an impact in returning to school. A close second factor is the "flexibility to take courses online" (37 percent).
> - **Current college students are more likely to consider alternative education paths.** The majority of current post-secondary students (68 percent) have considered alternative education programs (skills courses or micro-credentials), while only 42 percent of recent high school grads have considered it.
>
> "Cost remains the top barrier to higher education," by Laura Ascione, eSchoolMedia & eSchool News, October 19, 2021.

leaning independents with similar levels of education to believe that personal and intellectual growth should be the main purpose of college.

Along with Democrats and those who have progressed beyond a bachelor's degree, younger adults (those ages 18 to 29) are more likely than older adults to feel that personal and intellectual growth should be the primary purpose of college: some 43% of 18- to 29-year olds feel this way, compared with roughly one-third of those in older age groups.

In addition, Americans who themselves work in the education field tend to place a greater emphasis on personal and intellectual growth as the primary purpose of college: 46% believe that this should be the main purpose of a college degree, while 35% believe that college should mainly be a place to develop specific skills and knowledge (19% of those who work in the education industry consider them equally important).

Most College Graduates Regard Their College Experience as Very Useful for Intellectual Growth; Views Are More Mixed When It Comes to Job Opportunities and Marketable Skills

When asked to assess certain aspects of their own educational experience, about six-in-ten (62%) college graduates (including those who graduated from a two-year degree program) feel that their time in college was very useful in helping them grow personally and intellectually. About half say their college experience was very useful in helping them access job opportunities (53%) or in helping them develop skills and knowledge they could use in the workplace (49%).

The further people have progressed in their college career, the more likely they are to consider their experience very useful. Those with a postgraduate or professional degree are more likely to say that their college education was very useful in each of these respects compared with four-year degree holders, who are in turn more likely than those with a two-year associate degree to say that their education was very useful across each of these measures. For example, while two-thirds of those with a postgraduate or professional degree say their college education was very useful in opening doors to job opportunities, 56% of those with a four-year degree, and an even smaller share (40%) among those with a two-year degree, say the same. And while 57% of those with more than a bachelor's degree say college was very useful in helping them develop marketable skills, about half or a smaller share among those with a four- or two-year degree hold this view (49% and 43%, respectively).

When it comes to helping them grow professionally and intellectually, majorities of those with a postgraduate or professional degree (77%) and those with a bachelor's degree (64%) say college was very useful, compared with 46% of those with a two-year college degree.

Americans Have Mixed Views About the Extent to Which College Prepares Students for a Well-Paying Job in Today's Economy

When asked a broader set of questions about the impact of college more generally, the public expresses somewhat mixed views about the extent to which a college education prepares students for success in the workforce.

Two-thirds of Americans (67%) think that a traditional four-year degree prepares students for a well-paying job in today's economy at least somewhat well, but just 16% think it prepares them very well, and 29% think it does not prepare them well. A somewhat smaller share of Americans (58%) think that a two-year community college degree prepares students for a well-paying job either very (12%) or somewhat (46%) well, while 38% think that these programs do not prepare students well.

Interestingly, Americans with a four-year college degree are generally no more positive—or negative—than those with less education about the relationship between a four-year degree and a well-paying job: 13% of those with a bachelor's degree or more education say a four-year degree prepares people very well, as do 11% of those with a two-year associate degree, 12% of those with some college experience but no degree, and 17% of those with a high school diploma. Among those who did not complete high school, however, 40% believe that a four-year college degree does a very good job of preparing people for a well-paying job.

When it comes to assessments of a two-year college degree, about one-in-six (16%) Americans who hold this type of degree say it prepares workers very well for a well-paying job. This is considerably larger than the share of those with at least a bachelor's degree (7%) who say a two-year degree prepares people very well, but not necessarily more positive than the views of those with less education.

Blacks and Hispanics are more likely than whites to say four- and two-year degrees prepare people very well for a job in today's economy. For example, about three-in-ten (29%) Hispanics and about a quarter (24%) of blacks say this about a four-year degree, compared with 12% of whites. And while about one-in-five blacks and Hispanics (18% each) say a two-year associate degree prepares people very well, one-in-ten whites share this view.

These findings are consistent with previous Pew Research Center surveys that found that black and Latino parents view college as more essential for their children's success than do white parents.

A substantially larger share of the public has positive attitudes towards certification programs in a professional, technical or vocational field in the context of workforce development. Some 78% of Americans think that these programs prepare students well for a job in today's economy, including 26% who think they prepare students very well. Just roughly one-in-five (19%) think they do not prepare students well. It is important to note, however, that respondents were not asked about the effectiveness of certification programs *instead* of a college education.

Positive assessments of certificate programs as a way to prepare workers for jobs in today's economy are particularly widespread among those who did not complete high school; 44% in this group say these types of programs prepare people very well, compared with about a quarter (27%) of those with a high school diploma and a similar share of those with some college, but no degree (22%), a two-year degree (28%), or a four-year degree or more education (22%). Certificate programs are also particularly well-regarded among Hispanics, 39% of whom say they prepare people very well for a good job in today's economy. About a quarter of blacks (25%) and whites (23%) say the same.

One-Third of Americans Without a Bachelor's Degree Have Elected to Not Apply for a Job They Felt They Were Qualified for Because It Required a Four-Year Degree

Recent research has argued that there is a "credentials gap" in today's workforce, as employers increasingly require a bachelor's degree for positions that did not demand this level of schooling in the past. And the survey finds that 33% of Americans who do not have a four-year college degree report that they have declined to apply for a job they felt they were qualified for, because it required a bachelor's degree.

Americans who have engaged in some type of formal education beyond high school (short of obtaining a bachelor's degree) are particularly likely to believe they've been adversely affected by credentialing requirements as they work their way up the educational ladder. Some 25% of Americans with a high school diploma or less and no additional schooling beyond that have not applied for a job because of a bachelor's degree requirement. But that figure rises to 34% among those with a high school diploma plus additional vocational schooling, to 38% among those with some college experience but no degree, and to 44% among those with a two-year associate degree.

Put somewhat differently, as people receive additional formal education without actually obtaining a bachelor's degree, they may develop relevant skills without the on-paper credentials to match.

In addition, adults younger than 50 are much more likely than older adults to have refrained from applying to a job they felt they were qualified for because they didn't meet the formal educational requirements. About four-in-ten non-college graduates ages 18 to 29 (41%) and ages 30 to 49 (44%) say this has happened, compared with 31% of those ages 50 to 64 and just 12% of those 65 and older.

VIEWPOINT

> "In the U.S. one of the main reasons behind the decline in college enrollment and attendance is the high cost of college education."

Reasons Not to Go to College
Imed Bouchrika

In this viewpoint, Imed Bouchrika explains the factors driving decreasing college enrollment. Among the variety of factors that influence attendance at institutions of higher education are rising costs, with the average price of tuition rising dramatically. Coupled with the fact that over 14 percent of high school students are at schools where the majority of students are low income, and schools have been disrupted by the COVID-19 pandemic, it is no surprise that college enrollment has declined, especially among students facing economic and social barriers. Imed Bouchrika is the chief data scientist for Research.com.

As you read, consider the following questions:

1. What is the viewpoint's thesis?
2. What factors contribute to low college enrollment rates, according to Bouchrika?
3. How did students respond to the pandemic's impact on their college education?

"Reasons Not to Go to College: 52 Statistics on Barriers to Tertiary Education," by Imed Bouchrika, Research.com, May 14, 2023. Reprinted by permission.

33

While some students are bent on attending college and even endure AP vs dual enrollment to get a head start, others are hindered by certain circumstances to continue their education.

Despite the increase in enrollment rate in some regions and countries, the growing population of students who are not pursuing higher education is becoming more apparent. In the U.S., one of the main reasons behind the decline in college enrollment and attendance is the high cost of college education (College Board, 2019). Even with the attraction of the most beautiful colleges in the U.S., the cost will be a barrier to students who want to enroll. In fact, the rapidly increasing costs of higher education are causing widespread anxiety about student loans among American households, including an emerging concern of a likely higher education "bubble" (Reilly 2011, cited in Hemelt & Marcotte, 2016). These circumstances can be considered as reasons why you should not go to college.

High Cost of College

- For in-state tuition and fees at public four-year institutions, the average total tuition fee for the school year 2019–2020 is $21,950, including room and board charges. And even if students are granted financial aid, they still need to ask, "Does FAFSA cover off campus housing?"
- Average out-of-state tuition and fees at public four-year institutions increased by 2.4%, which brings the total charges to $38,330 for the school year 2019–2020.
- The tuition and fees for the school year 2019–2020 at private nonprofit four-year institutions rose by 3.4%, bringing the average total charges to $49,870.
- From 2009 to 2020, the published cost of in-state tuition and fees at four-year public institutions has increased at an average rate of 2.2% annually beyond inflation.
- For in-state students attending four-year public institutions and living on campus, 39% of their total budget is allotted to tuition and fees.

Poverty

According to Taylor (2005), poverty in the U.S. disproportionately affects African American and Latino students. African American and Latino children are more likely to attend high-poverty schools (National Center for Education Statistics, 2004).

- More than 14% of the nation's high school students, or about 1.8 million teenagers, attend schools where at least three-quarters live in poverty (GAO, 2018).
- 17% of high schools in the U.S. in the school year 2015–2016 were considered high-poverty schools (GAO, 2018).

Based on education data for the school year 2015–2016, the U.S. Government Accountability Office (GAO) found that students who attended relatively poor and small schools were less likely to have access to courses that could help them prepare for college (GAO, 2018). This lack of access to college preparatory courses can be considered as one of the reasons to not go to school. When it comes to higher education enrollment rates, students from low-income households lag behind students from high-income households by a large margin; conversely, economically-challenged students are more likely than their rich counterparts to drop out of school after enrolling (Aud et al., 2013, cited in Cilesiz & Drotos, 2016).

- The access to advanced placement courses such as calculus and physics decreased as the level of school poverty increased.
- Four-year public college institutions expect student applicants to have completed three to four math and science credits in high school.

In other parts of the globe, poverty also plays a key role in preventing a significant portion of the population from having access to tertiary education, among other reasons like gender discrimination, political conflict, and disabilities.

- In all countries (except high-income countries in Europe and North America), only 18 of the poorest youth for every 100 of the richest youth graduate from high school (GEM Report,

2020), and an even smaller number has the opportunity to go to college.

Gender

Despite the global effort for education to be accessible to all, there still are countries where women are marginalized (OECD Better Life Index, n.d.):

- There are at least 20 countries, mainly in Sub-Saharan Africa, where young women from rural areas cannot complete secondary school (GEM Report, 2020), much less have access to tertiary education.

An interesting reversal of the historical pattern, however, is witnessed in the countries that belong to the Organization for Economic Cooperation and Development (OECD). OECD is an international organization currently made up of 37 countries whose contributions to the improvement of global education include helping individuals and nations identify and develop the knowledge and skills to improve employment, personal and financial status, as well as promote social inclusion. In the majority of OECD countries, the percentage of women who complete tertiary education is higher than men (OECD, n.d.).

- 39% of women in most OECD countries between the ages of 25 and 64 are more likely to have a college degree compared to 33% of men in the same age range.

Disability

According to Wodon and Alasuutari (2018), there are more than 1 billion people around the world who experience some form of disability. Depending on the severity, a disability can place an individual at a disadvantage when it comes to enrolling and completing their education, especially if there are no facilities and educators who are properly equipped to cater to the needs of students with disabilities. This lack of proper facilities and educators can be considered as a reason for not going to college.

In the U.S., the National Longitudinal Transition Study-2 (NLTS2) conducted a study on students reported to have disabilities to help develop an understanding of their postsecondary experiences. The study which covers student data from 2001 to 2009 yielded the following results (Newman et al., 2011):

- 60% of young adults with disabilities were reported to have continued on to post-secondary education within an eight-year period after graduating from high school.
- Only 19% of young adults with disabilities were reported to have enrolled in 4-year colleges or universities.

Meanwhile, in some countries, the practice of segregation continues to exist.

- An average of 26% of adolescents with disabilities are out of school in six countries (UNESCO Institute for Statistics, 2018).

Military Service and Conflict Areas

In some countries, enlistment in the armed forces also affects a student's decision to pursue college or not.

- As of 2012, 56% of U.S. military service members had a high school education compared to the 30% who had some college education (Lauff et al., 2018).
- Only 17% of students with military service had earned a bachelor's degree in 2012 compared to 36% of students who did not serve in the military (Lauff et al., 2018).

In conflict areas across the globe, the opportunity for children to obtain college education has been cut short at the primary and secondary levels.

- According to UNICEF, 17 million school-age children and youth are refugees in countries hit by conflicts.
- In Yemen, more than 1,200 academic institutions have been damaged by the conflict and occupied by armed groups (Coughlan, 2018).

- In Uganda, 82% of the 1.5 million refugees are women and children whose access to education has been cut because of the war.
- Syria's "lost generation" is made up of 335,000 children who have missed out on education for years after they became refugees in Jordan (Coughlan, 2018).
- In Nigeria, Boko Haram violence has displaced 1.8 million people, including school-age children (Coughlan, 2018).

The COVID-19 Pandemic

In 2020, the coronavirus outbreak has taken a massive toll not only on the source of livelihood of people around the world but also on education. The coronavirus pandemic has created a worldwide higher education crisis (Raaper & Brown, 2020). The pandemic definitely falls under the category of unique debate topics for reasons not to attend college, especially with the availability of distance learning options. In the U.S., for example, higher education leaders were able to quickly transition students to remote learning in order to complete the 2019 academic year. The bigger challenge, however, is when and how to open the academic year of 2020 in the face of COVID-19 (Kim et al., 2020).

In a survey conducted by the American Council on Education, 192 presidents of higher education institutions in the U.S. were asked to choose the most pressing concerns they have, including their institutions' capacity and needs in the face of the COVID-19 pandemic (Turk et al., 2020).

- 86% of presidents claim that their biggest concern is the number of fall and summer enrollment.
- 65% of presidents state that they are worried about long-term financial viability.
- 54% of presidents at public four-year institutions are most concerned about providing emergency aid to students.

- Meanwhile, 45% of presidents at private four-year institutions choose "laying off faculty and/or staff" as the third pressing issue they have.
- 49% of presidents are considering merging or eliminating academic programs as part of the actions they might deem necessary to take.

In a recent survey by OneClass, more than 10,839 students from 255 colleges and universities in the U.S. share how COVID-19 has directly affected their pursuit of college education (OneClass Blog, 2020):

- 50.9% of respondents reveal that they are facing tuition financing problems.
- 41.8% of respondents claim that they have not been negatively affected by the pandemic.
- 7.3% of the students are "changing gears" and do something else.
- 1.5% of students who can no longer afford their tuition are leaving college to seek full-time employment.

Because of the coronavirus pandemic, it can thus be anticipated that the ongoing disintegration of the higher education's social and physical environments will have a considerable impact on students and that the most adversely affected will be those from disadvantaged households (Montacute, 2020).

The Future of College Education

COVID-19 has impacted 80% of the world's student population with nearly 60 million of previously enrolled college students currently dealing with disruption in their studies (Martin & Furiv, 2020). While there are colleges and universities that are capable of providing their students with online education, this option is not applicable to the majority of higher education institutions, especially in countries that are not economically prepared to address not only the ongoing but the aftereffects of COVID-19.

With the employment rate also facing its own crisis due to the pandemic, students are dealt with an even tougher challenge. Besides, there are companies that don't require a degree, making it seem reasonable to not finish a degree at all.

Nevertheless, just recently, the UNESCO International Institute for Educational Planning launched an international research project, which aims to help countries identify possible policies and instruments supporting flexible learning pathways or FLPs. But with the pandemic still ongoing, the implementation of possible proposed actions will have to wait. Meanwhile, it is a good idea to stay motivated with these employee engagement quotes (https://research.com/education/reasons-not-to-go-to-college) that are suitable for students, too, as opportunities to study may present themselves.

References

Cilesiz, S., & Drotos, S.M. (2016). High-poverty urban high school students' plans for higher education. *Urban Education, 51* (1), 3-31. https://doi.org/10.1177/0042085914543115

Textor, C. (2020. August 7). China: Tertiary education enrollment rate 2018. *Statista*.

College Board. (2019, November). Trends in college pricing 2019. *Trends in Higher Education Series*. New York, NY: The College Board.

Coughlan, S. (2018, September 5). Going back to school in a war zone. *BBC News*.

Dahir, A. L. (2017, January 5). Africa has too few universities for its fast growing population. *Quartz Africa*.

Darvas, P., Gao, S., Shen, Y., & Bawany, B. (2017, October 27). *Sharing higher education's promise beyond the few in Sub-Saharan Africa (English)*. Washington, DC: The World Bank.

Duffin, E. (2020, February 12). U.S. higher education enrollment rates, by age group 2018. *Statista*.

GPE (2020, May 28). Education data highlights. *Global Partnership for Education*.

EducationData (2020, April 12). Student loan debt statistics. *EducationData.org*.

EuroStat (2020, March 11). Tertiary education statistics. *Statistics Explained*. Luxemburg: EuroStat.

Federal Reserve Bank of New York. (2019, February 6). *The Labor market for recent college graduates*. New York, NY: Federal Reserve Bank of New York.

Fleet, J. V. (2012, September 17). Africa's education crisis: In school but not learning. *Brookings*.

Fleet, J. V., Watkins, K., & Greubel, L. (2012, September 17). Africa learning barometer. *Brookings*.

GAO (2018, October 11). *K-12 education: Public high schools with more students in poverty and smaller schools provide fewer academic offerings to prepare for college.* Washington, DC: U.S. Government Accountability Office.

GAO (2018). *Public high schools with more students in poverty and smaller schools provide fewer academic offerings to prepare for college (GAO-19-8).* Washington, DC: U.S. Government Accountability Office.

Hemelt, S.W., & Marcotte, D.E. (2016). The changing landscape of tuition and enrollment in American public higher education. *Russell Sage Foundation Journal of the Social Sciences, 2* (1), 42-68. http://www.jstor.com/stable/10.7758/rsf.2016.2.1.03

IAU. (2020). *The impact of COVID-19 on higher education worldwide.* Paris, France: International Association of Universities.

Kim, H., Krishnan, C., Law, J., & Rounsaville, T. (2020, May 21). *COVID-19 and US higher education enrollment: Preparing leaders for fall.* New York, NY: McKinsey & Company.

Lauff, E., Chen, X., & Morgan, T. (2018). *Military service and educational attainment of high school sophomores after 9/11.* Washington, DC: NCES.

Martin, M., & Furiv, U. (2020, March 28). COVID-19 shows the need to make learning more flexible. *University World News.*

Montacute, R. (2020). *Social mobility and Covid-19. Implications of the Covid-19 crisis for educational inequality.* SuttonTrust

Moore, M. (2020, March 25). Tertiary education in Asia Pacific – statistics & facts. *Statista.*

Moore, M. (2020, March 3). APAC: Number of people enrolled in tertiary education by country 2018. *Statista.* Retrieved June 28, 2020, from

Nadworny, E. (2019, December 16). Fewer students are going to college. Here's why that matters. *NPR.org.*

NCES (2019). Percentage of the population 3 to 34 years old enrolled in school, by age group: Selected years, 1940 through 2018. *2019 Tables & Figures.* Washington, DC: NCES.

Newman, L., Wagner, M., Knokey, A. M., Marder, C., Nagle, K., Shaver, D., Wei, X., with Cameto, R., Contreras, E., Ferguson, K., Greene, S., Schwarting, M. (2011). *The post-high school outcomes of young adults with disabilities up to 8 years after high school: A report from the National Longitudinal Transition Study-2 (NLTS2)* (NCSER 2011-3005). Menlo Park: SRI International.

NSC Research Center (2019, Fall). *Current Term Enrollment Estimates Fall 2019.* Washington, DC: National Student Clearinghouse.

NSC Research Center (2019, December 16). *Fall 2019 Current Term Enrollment Estimates.* Washington, DC: National Student Clearinghouse.

OECD (n.d.). Education. *OECD Better Life Index.* Paris, France: OECD.

OneClass Blog. (2020, June 1). How has the pandemic affected your ability to afford school? *OneClass.*

Roser, M., & Ortiz-Ospina, E. (2013). Gross enrollment ratio in tertiary education. *Our World in Data.*

Pasquali, M. (2019, July 11). Mexico: students in higher education 2009-2018. *Statista.*

StatCan (2020, February 19). Postsecondary enrolments, by registration status, institution type, status of student in Canada and gender. *Statistics Canada.*

Raaper, R., & Brown, C. (2020). The Covid-19 pandemic and the dissolution of the university campus: implications for student support practice. *Journal of Professional Capital and Community*, (Vol. and No. ahead-of-print). https://doi.org/10.1108/JPCC-06-2020-0032

Salmi, J. (2018, November). All around the world – Higher education equity policies across the globe. *World Access to Higher Education.*

Taylor, J. A. (2005). Poverty and student achievement. *Multicultural Education, 12* (4), 53. Gale Academic OneFile.

World Bank (2017, October 5). *Tertiary education.* Washington, DC: World Bank.

Turk, J., Soler Salazar, M. C., & Vigil, D. (2020, April 23). *College and University presidents respond to COVID-19: April 2020 survey.* Washington, DC: American Council on Education.

UIS-UNESCO. (n.d.). Enrollment by level of education. *UIS Statistics.*

UNESCO GEM Report. (2015). Humanitarian aid for education: Why it matters and why more is needed. *Education for All Global Monitoring Report. Policy Paper 21 (21).* Paris, France: UNESCO.

UNESCO (2018). Education and disability: Analysis of data from 49 countries. *Information Paper N. 49,* March 2018. UIS-UNESCO

UNESCO (n.d.). Tertiary completion rate. *World Inequality Database on Education.*

UNESCO (n.d.). Higher education attendance. *World Inequality Database on Education.*

VIEWPOINT 3

> "The benefits of higher education come in the form of higher wages, increased productivity, and positive social outcomes... high levels of student debt can also harm certain sectors of the economy and lower the net wealth of households."

The Effect of Student Debt on the Economy
Peter G. Peterson Foundation

In this viewpoint from the Peter G. Peterson Foundation, the authors assert that in considering the impact of student debt, policymakers must consider not only its drawbacks, but also the benefits of higher education. The drawbacks of student debt include lower home ownership, lowered net worth, barriers to small business formation, and lower consumer spending among others. Meanwhile, the economic benefits of higher education include higher wages, increased productivity, stable employment and related improvements in quality of life, as well as a "knowledge spillover" effect. When this viewpoint was written, policy makers in the Biden Administration were considering potential reforms such as loan forgiveness in the short term, and other solutions in the long term. The Peter G. Peterson Foundation is an American nonprofit organization dedicated to addressing America's long-term fiscal challenges.

"How Does Student Debt Affect The Economy?," Peter G. Peterson Foundation, September 7, 2021. Reprinted by permission.

As you read, consider the following questions:
1. What are the drawbacks of student debt?
2. What are the ethical implications of the high levels of student debt in the U.S.?
3. How is the federal government considering short- and long-term solutions to student debt?

The Biden Administration recently extended the pause on federal student loan repayments through January 31, 2022 and forgave $5.8 billion in loans for 300,000 borrowers who have a total or permanent disability. At the same time, advocates are calling for more long-term and comprehensive solutions to the growing amount of student debt. Proposals such as a regulatory restructuring of repayment plans and cancellation of student debt through personal bankruptcy or other means have been offered as reforms to address the growing student debt burden.

As policymakers consider such proposals, it's important to understand the positive and negative effects of student debt on the economy. Student debt in the United States currently stands at about $1.73 trillion; it is the second-highest category of household debt, next to mortgage debt, with the average borrower owing an estimated $39,000 in loan repayments. What's more, such debt has grown significantly over the past several years—the amount of outstanding student debt has nearly doubled since 2011.

In general, achieving higher education supports broad economic as well as individual benefits, including a more productive workforce and higher wages. Financing one's education through loans may enable students to enroll in post-secondary education and achieve those outcomes. However, as overall student debt has grown over the past decade, it is apparent that such borrowing can place a financial burden on households and has harmful effects on homeownership rates and small business formation.

What Are the Economic Benefits of Higher Education?

Data shows that in the aggregate, higher education produces financial and social benefits for graduates and their communities, such as higher wages, stable employment, increased productivity, and improved quality of life.

Despite rising tuition costs in recent years, the rate of return on a college education remains high at around 14 percent, substantially surpassing benchmarks for other secure investments such as the return on long-term stocks or bonds. Those with college and advanced degrees see this return in the form of higher wages. Some estimates indicate college graduates experience a 75 percent earnings premium, on average, over those with a high school diploma, or approximately $30,000 more annually.

Those with higher degrees of education are also generally less likely to experience unemployment or underemployment. In 2020, the unemployment rate for those with a high school diploma and no college education was nearly twice as high as for those with a bachelor's degree.

Higher education also has important societal effects. There is evidence of a "knowledge spillover" in which the presence of more educated workers increases the productivity of others. That additional productivity translates into higher wages for those who did not finish high school, high school graduates, and other college graduates, according to research published in the *American Economic Review*.

There is further research to support claims that having a more educated populace lowers crime and incarceration rates, and that college graduates generally report more positive life outcomes in terms of happiness, health, civic participation, and financial security.

How Does Student Debt Harm the Economy?

Although many positive effects of attaining higher education exist, there are also some negative implications of the accumulation of student debt. In particular, such debt may impede economic growth in the long-run by slowing spending across certain sectors and by destabilizing personal savings typically used to survive significant financial events, such as economic recessions and retirement.

Student Debt Reduces Home Ownership

Homeownership rates have been falling steadily since the Great Recession, but especially among young Americans in their 20s and 30s, who experienced nearly twice the decline in homeownership rates as the general population between 2005 and 2014. A study published by the Federal Reserve reported that student debt accounted for around 20 percent of that decline and precluded 400,000 young adults from buying homes over that period.

Student Debt Reduces Net Worth

Student debt may also jeopardize household finances and leave borrowers worse off financially than previous generations. A 2013 study by the Federal Reserve found that on average, households with student debt had a lower net worth ($42,800) than those without ($117,700). In fact, 41 percent of households headed by someone age 25–38 owed student debt in 2019; in 1989, that number was only 15 percent. The prevalence and amount of student debt owed by young adults today may be associated with why such adults hold less wealth than previous generations did at that age. In 2019, millennials only held 4 percent of the nation's wealth but in 1989, when baby boomers were approximately the same age as today's millennials, they held 21 percent of total wealth.

That lower net worth can also make it harder for households to weather economic downturns. For example, households holding student debt during the Great Recession experienced a larger decline in their net worth (a 12 percent drop) over that period than those who did not hold any student debt (9 percent).

Student Debt Hurts Small Businesses

Growing student debt levels are also hampering small business formation, particularly for firms that rely on personal capital injections for growth. According to a 2015 paper from the

Philadelphia Federal Reserve, an increase in student debt of approximately 3.3 percent resulted in a 14.4 percent decrease in the formation of small firms (defined as having 1 to 4 employees) at the county level between 2000 and 2010.

Other Effects
Student debt can have other negative effects on the economy and individuals. For example, a 2014 study showed that monthly student loan repayments impeded family formation in the years immediately following college graduation for bachelor degree-holding women. Other research suggests that student loan repayments slow consumer spending, inhibit saving for retirement, and lower access to future credit due to higher delinquency rates.

Conclusion
Student debt can have both positive and negative effects on the economy. The benefits of higher education come in the form of higher wages, increased productivity, and positive social outcomes —making degree attainment a high-return investment. At the same time, high levels of student debt can also harm certain sectors of the economy and lower the net wealth of households. Those tradeoffs will be important as policymakers continue to debate student loan reforms.

VIEWPOINT 4

> "A one-size-fits-all approach to assisting students and their families with post-secondary financial planning (e.g., a single financial aid presentation for all families) is inadequate to meet the diversity of needs."

Removing Financial Barriers to Higher Education and Career Success

Timothy A. Poynton, Richard T. Lapan, and Amanda M. Marcotte

In this excerpted viewpoint, the authors explain how the rising costs of higher education have become a key challenge for students and their families, not only with increases in tuition but also prices for room and board on campus, at both public and private colleges and universities. An online survey found that demographic, academic, motivational, and career factors interacted with financial factors as students moved from high school to college. Financial literacy and career development services thus play a critical role in promoting student success. Timothy A. Poynton is an associate professor in the department of counseling and school psychology at University of Massachusetts Boston. Richard T. Lapan is a professor and Amanda M. Marcotte is an associate professor in the department of student development at University of Massachusetts Amherst.

"Financial Planning Strategies of High School Seniors: Removing Barriers to Career Success," by Poynton, Timothy A., Lapan, R. T, Marcotte, A. M, *The Career Development Quarterly*.2015. Reprinted by permission.

As you read, consider the following questions:

1. How much did undergraduate tuition, room, and board at colleges increase between 2000–2001 and 2010–2011?
2. What key factors influence high school seniors' plans for financing their college education?
3. How can high school counselors better support high school seniors in financial planning?

This study explored the postsecondary financial planning of graduating 12th graders as a barrier to educational and career decision making and success. Seniors planning on pursuing postsecondary education (N = 744) from 16 high schools completed an online survey measuring their plans for financing their postsecondary education. They also provided information regarding their academic achievement, motivation, certainty, and postsecondary goals and plans. Students clustered into 4 distinct financial planning strategy groups. These financial planning clusters were evident across a diverse sample of high schools. Almost half of all graduating 12th graders had limited financial planning strategies. Groupings and strategies employed by students were significantly related to career development theory and research. The critical role for career development services in promoting student success is discussed.

The cost of postsecondary education has risen sharply, making it one of the most important challenges to the college and career decision-making process for students and their families. The National Center for Education Statistics (NCES, 2012) reported that between the 2000–2001 and 2010–2011 academic years, the prices for undergraduate tuition and room and board increased 42% at public institutions and 31% at private not-for-profit institutions—after adjustment for inflation. Since 2008, Sallie Mae (2012) has conducted annual surveys of college students and their parents that focus on the types of funding sources utilized (e.g., family savings plans, scholarships, loans), the actual amount associated with each funding type, and the college decision-making process. In the 2011–2012 academic year, 69% of students reported eliminating a college they were accepted to because of cost—a figure that has increased annually since 2009, when 56% of students reported eliminating a college they were accepted to because of cost. This reality is being felt and responded to by students across the socioeconomic spectrum. For example, there has been an increase in students from families that earn more than $100,000 a year who are deciding to live at home while attending college as a cost-saving measure—from 24% in 2010 to 47% in 2012 (Sallie Mae, 2012).

The financing of postsecondary education as a barrier to educational and career success has become a focus for career development theory and research. For example, Lent (2013a) argued that one of the most useful aspects of social cognitive career theory (SCCT) is that it can be employed to help people develop the "career-life preparedness" skills necessary to minimize barriers and strengthen supports for educational and career attainment. Financing postsecondary education is, in the SCCT choice model, one of the most challenging proximal environmental influences affecting the setting and implementation of career choice goals (Lent, 2013b).

Previous and emerging research support this emphasis on finances as a major impediment to the career choices and success of college students (Lent, Brown, Talleyrand, & McPartland, 2002), including career choices in science, technology, engineering, and math (Fouad et al., 2010). McWhirter and her colleagues have consistently identified funding for postsecondary education (e.g., loans, financial aid, and scholarships) as one of the most critical barriers to career success, especially for minority women (McWhirter, Torres, Salgado, & Valdez, 2007) and lower income and underrepresented Latina/o youth (McWhirter, Luginbuhl, & Brown, 2014). Furthermore, a lack of financial planning and pre- paredness has been linked to greater rates of dropping out of college (Ishitani & DesJardins, 2002). Students with greater financial need are less likely to persist at their chosen schools (Wessel, Bell, McPherson, Costello, & Jones, 2006), and the difference between what the financial aid students expect to receive versus what they actually receive shapes college choice, access, and success (Kim, DesJardins, & McCall, 2009). Increasing high school seniors' readiness for, access to, and graduation from postsecondary education has become a leading national priority (U.S. Department of Education, 2010). Research has made significant progress in better understanding potentially malleable factors that promote successful postsecondary transitions for graduating high school seniors (for a review, see Lapan, Turner, & Pierce, 2012). Interdisciplinary research has found that the readiness to succeed in college (i.e., access, retention, performance, and graduation) relates strongly to demographic, academic, motivational, and career planning factors. Demographic factors such as sex, ethnic minority status, socioeconomic status (SES), and speaking languages other than English at home are consistently associated with postsecondary outcomes. For example, bachelor's degree completion rates among eighth graders who aspire to at least a 4-year degree are higher for women than for men, and for Asian American students when compared with students of all other ethnicities (Trusty & Niles, 2004). Female high school students may anticipate more barriers to financing postsecondary education than male students, and Mexican American high school students anticipate encountering more barriers to postsecondary success than White high school students (McWhirter et al., 2007). When predicting Holland types of college students with declared majors, a three-way interaction exists among gender, SES, and ethnic minority status (Trusty, Ng, & Plata, 2000). Spending more time working on high school assignments, earning good grades, and taking demanding courses that hold students to high academic standards are academic-related skills necessary for postsecondary success (American College Testing, 2007).

Purpose of the Study

Motivational factors such as achievement motivation, connectedness, a sense of personal belonging in school, interpersonal relationships and skills, and perceptions of safety are strongly linked to critical markers of student postsecondary success. These markers include college grade point average (GPA) and retention, as well as lower rates of risky in- school and out-of-school behaviors such as drug use and driving while intoxicated (e.g., Centers for Disease Control and Prevention [CDC], 2009; Lapan, Wells, Petersen, & McCann, 2014; Robbins et al., 2004). Meanwhile, career planning and development attitudes, behaviors, and decisions (e.g., short- and long-term educational goals, certainty, completing a free application for federal student aid [FAFSA], and applying to multiple colleges—especially for students with more marginal academic records) explain unique and meaningful portions of the variance in successful transitions to postsecondary education and persistence to graduation (Allen & Robbins, 2010; Lent, 2013b; Roderick, Nagaoka, Coca, & Moeller, 2008).

Therefore, our study examined how graduating 12th graders plan to finance their postsecondary education and assessed the extent to which career development factors linked in prior research to college and career readiness influence and interact with these financial plans. Research has demonstrated how demographic, academic, motivational, and career planning factors influence and interact with career planning and postsecondary success. However, the role of financial planning in career planning and postsecondary success has not been comprehensively examined. We expected that the specific approaches to financing postsecondary education adopted by graduating 12th graders would reveal clusters of students based on these plans, given prior research linking demographic factors to career planning and postsecondary success. Furthermore, we expected that these clusters would differ on academic, motivational, and career planning factors in ways similar to previous research linking these factors to postsecondary success. Having an increased research-driven understanding of the role of financial planning in the high school-to-college transition would greatly assist educational leaders and policy makers to design more effective systems of support for both students and their families.

[…]

Implications for Practice

Our study extends prior research to increase the understanding of how graduating 12th graders plan to meet the barrier of financing their postsecondary education. Graduating high school seniors cluster into distinct groups based on what approaches they expect to use to successfully negotiate and master this challenge. These divergent groups do not occur in only certain kinds of high schools (e.g., high- or low-achieving urban, suburban, or rural schools). Instead, strong heterogeneity in financial planning strategies for students was evident in 15 out of the 16 high schools sampled, and, in every high school, at least 25% of the students were members of Group 2 (13th Graders). This finding strongly suggests that a one-size-fits-all approach to assisting students and their families with postsecondary financial planning (e.g., a single financial aid presentation for all families) is inadequate to meet the diversity of needs.

Instead, counselors and career development practitioners in our high schools and postsecondary institutions need to proactively deliver differentiated support services that are responsive to the diverse range of financing approaches being adopted by students. Findings from our study suggest the following strategy to identify financial planning group membership and specific intervention implementation. First, anticipate finding students to be members of all four groups. With this mindset, a short and transparent survey could be used to collect the following information from students: parents' levels of education, grades, the number of AP classes taken, the number of colleges applied to, engagement in and a positive attitude toward school, certainty about a plan for postsecondary education, and the 12 items we employed to assess students' financial plans. With this information, each student can be placed in one of the four financial planning groups described in our study. Once students have been identified in terms of which group they represent, specific interventions can be implemented to assist them. For example, First Generation students are doing well in school and are mostly on their own to pay for their education. Although they are planning to use loans, these students are hopeful and counting on scholarships to substantially offset their expenses. Prior research suggests that First Generation students are at risk for dropping out of college as their debt escalates from one year to the next and scholarship money does not come through in the amounts needed (Kim et al., 2009; Wessel et al., 2006). First Generation students may not be aware of all of the options available to them or maintain the level of perceived efficacy needed to cope with this barrier to their career futures. Effective advisement and counseling at both the high school and postsecondary levels (e.g., developing a plan to finance postsecondary education while the student is still in high school, providing proactive financial counseling in college, and providing the emotional and problem-solving supports needed to develop more adaptive financial planning strategies) would increase the likelihood that First Generation students would persist. The goal of career counseling would be to minimize the barriers and maximize supports for First Generation students and their families (Lent, 2013a). Of great concern, 13th Graders have some of the same difficulties that led the W. T. Grant Foundation (1988) to identify the needs of the young people not bound for college, termed the forgotten half, as a national crisis. Although, on average, this cluster of students is in good academic standing, they are less certain about and committed to their postsecondary plans. Their lower level of academic engagement in high school and less positive attitude toward school in general make them more likely candidates to not complete the kinds of postsecondary training now essential for success in the labor market (Symonds, Schwartz, & Ferguson, 2011). As financial pressures mount and with limited financial resources from their families available to them, 13th Graders would likely face negative consequences as a result of not having a plan to pay for their education and having a less clear vision of their career future.

Career counseling professionals at both the high school and postsecondary levels could begin to help these 13th Graders by doing two things. First, every student should complete a FAFSA. Students who complete a FAFSA are more likely to attend a postsecondary educational institution and persist toward completion (for an annotated bibliography, see U.S. Department of Education, Office of Elementary and Secondary Education, 2011).

Second, counselors need to provide students with personalized career counseling services that help them identify with, commit to, and take ownership for succeeding in a vocational direction that both interests and means something important to them. Both of these objectives could be accomplished through the intentional implementation of the guidance curriculum and individual planning components of a comprehensive school counseling program model (Gysbers & Henderson, 2012). The career development needs of this half of our student population must not be forgotten.

More than 85% of the students in the Parent Reliant and Parent and Self-Reliant groups are expecting parents to pay for their postsecondary education. Students in both of these groups could benefit from developing an explicit understanding of the expectations their parents actually have of them—in terms of the amounts and types of loans (e.g., Stafford loans) parents anticipate their children will need to take out. For example, helping students to have direct conversations with their families about these issues would assist students who believe they will not have to take out any personal loans to confirm this assumption or develop a now agreed upon financing plan with their parents. Although students in the Parent and Self-Reliant group are expecting to accumulate loan debt themselves, it is important for students in both of these groups to have access to current information about federal, state, and private loan programs and information about scholarships and work-study opportunities. This information would assist students in both groups to adapt to any changes that adversely affect their family's ability to pay for large portions of their education (e.g., when the stock market fluctuates and available funds for parents diminish).

[…]

References

Allen, J., & Robbins, S. (2010). Effects of interest-major congruence, motivation, and academic performance on timely degree attainment. *Journal of Counseling Psychology, 57*, 23–35.

American College Testing. (2007). *Issues in college success: Impact of cognitive, psychosocial, and career factors on educational and workplace success.* Retrieved from http://www.act.org/research/policymakers/pdf/CognitiveNoncognitive.pdf

Centers for Disease Control and Prevention. (2009). *School connectedness: Strategies for increasing protective factors among youth.* Atlanta, GA: U.S. Department of Health and Human Services.

Fouad, N. A., Hackett, G., Smith, P. L., Kantamneni, N., Fitzpatrick, M., Haag, S., & Spencer, D. (2010). Barriers and supports for continuing in mathematics and science: Gender and educational level differences. *Journal of Vocational Behavior, 77*, 361–373.

Gysbers, N. C., & Henderson, P. (2012). *Developing and managing your school guidance & counseling program* (5th ed.). Alexandria, VA: American Counseling Association.

Ishitani, T. T., & DesJardins, S. L. (2002). A longitudinal investigation of dropout from college in the United States. *Journal of College Student Retention, 4*, 172–201.

Kim, J., DesJardins, S. L., & McCall, B. P. (2009). Exploring the effects of student expectations about financial aid on postsecondary choice: A focus on income and racial/ethnic differences. *Research in Higher Education, 50*, 741–774.

Lapan, R. T., Turner, S. L., & Pierce, M. E. (2012). College and career readiness: Policy and research to support effective counseling in schools. In N. A. Fouad, J. A. Carter, &

L. M. Subich (Eds.), *APA handbook of counseling psychology* (pp. 57–73). Washington, DC: American Psychological Association.

Lapan, R. T., Wells, R., Petersen, J., & McCann, L. A. (2014). Stand tall to protect students: School counselors strengthening school connectedness. *Journal of Counseling & Development, 92,* 304–315.

Lent, R. W. (2013a). Career-life preparedness: Revisiting career planning and adjustment in the new workplace. *The Career Development Quarterly, 61,* 2–14.

Lent, R. W. (2013b). Social cognitive career theory. In S. D. Brown and R. W. Lent (Eds.), *Career development and counseling: Putting theory and research to work* (pp. 115–146). Hoboken, NJ: Wiley.

Lent, R. W., Brown, S. D., Talleyrand, R., & McPartland, E. B. (2002). Career choice barriers, supports, and coping strategies: College students' experiences. *Journal of Vocational Behavior, 60,* 61–72.

McWhirter, E. W., Luginbuhl, P. J., & Brown, K. (2014). Apoyenos! Latina/o student recommendations for high school supports. *Journal of Career Development, 41,* 3–23. McWhirter, E. W., Torres, D. M., Salgado, S., & Valdez, M. (2007). Perceived barriers and postsecondary plans in Mexican American and White adolescents. *Journal of CareerAssessment, 15,* 119–138.

National Center for Education Statistics. (2012). *Digest of education statistics: 2011* (NCES 2012-001). Retrieved from http://nces.ed.gov/programs/digest/d11/ch_3.asp

Public Agenda. (2010). *Can I get a little advice here: How an overstretched high school guidance system is undermining students' college aspirations.* Retrieved from http://www.publicagenda.org/pages/can-i-get-a-little-advice-here

Robbins, S. B., Allen, J., Casillas, A., Peterson, C. H., & Le, H. (2006). Unraveling the differential effects of motivational and skills, social, and self-management measures from traditional predictors of college outcomes. *Journal of Educational Psychology, 98,* 598–616. Robbins, S. B., Lauver, K., Le, H., Davis, D., Langley, R., & Carlstrom, A. (2004). Do psychosocial and study skill factors predict college outcomes? A meta-analysis. *Psychological Bulletin, 130,* 261–288.

Roderick, M., Nagaoka, J., Coca, V., & Moeller, E. (2008). *From high school to the future: Potholes on the road to college.* Chicago, IL: Consortium on Chicago School Research at the University of Chicago. Retrieved from http://ccsr.uchicago.edu/sites/default/files/publications/CCSR_Potholes_Report.pdf

Sallie Mae. (2012). *How America pays for college 2012.* Retrieved from https://www.salliemae.com/plan-for-college/how-america-pays-for-college/

Sirin, S. R. (2005). Socioeconomic status and academic achievement: A meta-analytic review of research. *Review of Educational Research, 75,* 417–453.

Symonds, W. C., Schwartz, R. B., & Ferguson, R. (2011). *Pathways to prosperity: Meeting the challenge of preparing young Americans for the 21st century.* Retrieved from http://www.gse.harvard.edu/news/11/02/pathways-prosperity-meeting-challenge-preparing-young-americans-21st-century

Trusty, J., Ng, K., & Plata, M. (2000). Interaction effects of gender, SES, and race–ethnicity on postsecondary educational choices of U.S. students. *The Career Development Quarterly, 49,* 45–59.

Trusty, J., & Niles, S. G. (2004). Realized potential or lost talent: High school variables and bachelor's degree completion. *The Career Development Quarterly, 53,* 2–15.

U.S. Department of Education. (2010). Race to the top fund. Retrieved from http:// www2.ed.gov/programs/racetothetop/index.html

U.S. Department of Education, Office of Elementary and Secondary Education. (2011). *The FAFSA completion project: An annotated bibliography*. Washington, DC: Author.

Ward, J. H. (1963). Hierarchical grouping to optimize an objective function. *Journal of the American Statistical Association, 58,* 236–244.

Wessel, R. D., Bell, C. L., McPherson, J. D., Costello, M. T., & Jones, J. A. (2006). Academic disqualification and persistence to graduation by financial aid category and academic ability. *Journal of College Student Retention, 8,* 185–198.

W. T. Grant Foundation. (1988). *The forgotten half: Pathways to success for America's youth and young families.* New York, NY: Author.

Periodical and Internet Sources Bibliography

The following articles have been selected to supplement the diverse views presented in this chapter.

Douglas Belkin, "Americans Are Losing Faith in College Education, WSJ-NORC Poll Finds," *Wall Street Journal*, March 31, 2023. https://www.wsj.com/articles/americans-are-losing-faith-in-college-education-wsj-norc-poll-finds-3a836ce1.

Jessica Blake, "American Confidence in Higher Ed Hits Historic Low," *Inside Higher Education*, July 11, 2023. https://www.insidehighered.com/news/business/financial-health/2023/07/11/american-confidence-higher-ed-hits-historic-low.

Paulina Cachero, "Is College Worth It? Undergraduate Enrollment Slips in U.S.," *Bloomberg*, October 20, 2022. https://www.bloomberg.com/news/articles/2022-10-20/is-college-tuition-too-expensive-undergraduate-enrollment-drops-as-costs-rise?srnd=premium.

Andrew Delblanco, "The University Crisis: Does the Pandemic Mark a Breaking Point?" the *Nation*, February 7, 2022. https://www.thenation.com/article/society/american-universities-crisis/.

Christopher L. Eisgruber, "A College Degree Is Worth the Cost — And Then Some," *Washington Post*, April 26, 2023. https://www.washingtonpost.com/opinions/2023/04/26/college-degree-value-investment-return/.

Andrew Foote and Michel Grosz, "The Effect of Local Labor Market Downturns On Postsecondary Enrollment And Program Choice," *Education Finance and Policy*, October 1, 2020. https://doi.org/10.1162/edfp_a_00288.

Alyssa Fowers and Danielle Douglas-Gabrielle, "Who Has Student Loan Debt in America?" *Washington Post*, July 14, 2023. https://www.washingtonpost.com/education/2022/05/22/student-loan-borrowers/.

Denise Jackson and Michael Tomlinson, "Investigating the Relationship Between Career Planning, Proactivity And Employability Perceptions Among Higher Education Students In

Uncertain Labour Market Conditions," *High Education*, January 15, 2020. https://doi.org/10.1007/s10734-019-00490-5.

Ron Lieber and Tara Siegel Bernard, "After Supreme Court Rulings, Answering Reader Questions About Paying for College," *New York Times,* July 8, 2023. https://www.nytimes.com/2023/07/08/business/student-loans-college-admissions-supreme-court.html.

Joseph A. Rios, Guangming Ling, Robert Pugh, Dovid Becker, and Adam Bacall, "Identifying Critical 21st-Century Skills for Workplace Success: A Content Analysis of Job Advertisements," *Educational Researcher*, January 21, 2020. https://doi.org/10.3102/0013189X19890600.

OPPOSING VIEWPOINTS® SERIES

CHAPTER 2

Are There Suitable Alternatives to Traditional Higher Education?

Chapter Preface

An understanding of the value and purpose of a university education is important, as are other factors that should be considered when evaluating choices for post-secondary education in the U.S. Such choices include two-year community college degrees compared to a four-year bachelor's degree, or for-profit versus non-profit providers of higher education, or the possibility of alternative credentials such as badges and stackable credentials.

While four-year degrees are the gold standard for higher education, as the cost of college education rises, community college degrees have steadily gained traction, with 47 states in the U.S. offering low-cost or no-cost two-year degrees in the past few years.[1] Community colleges not only offer significant cost savings but offer an affordable way to transfer credits to a four-year institution leading to a bachelor's degree. Those choosing not to continue on to university often can obtain practical two-year degrees, allowing them to enter the workplace with marketable skills. However, the data on job prospects for community college graduates is mixed, and it is undeniable that community colleges offer less of a traditional college experience in terms of quality of student life.

Four-year colleges/universities can be non-profit or for-profit, with many potential students and their families lacking a clear understanding of the difference. Prospective students may find for-profits attractive due to their aggressive marketing and touted flexibility. While for-profit colleges may have advantages, what is often not clear to applicants are issues such as higher costs, higher student debt, lower graduation rates, and potential lack of degree acceptance in the marketplace.

In the U.S., certificates and stackable credentials were first offered in their current form in the 1970s.[2] Alternatives to traditional higher education such as certificates and badges have become increasingly popular due to no-cost sites and low-cost providers such as Coursera and LinkedIn, among others. Although badges and certificates often supplement college degrees, they can stand alone as credentials for career entry, as in Google's Project Management and UX Design. Stackable credentials offer many benefits, from cost and time saving to flexibility, customization, and career-relevance. However, these credentials do have drawbacks stemming from lack of acceptance by employers and lack of standardization in content.

This chapter addresses the above issues, presenting opposing viewpoints on two-year and four-year institutions of higher education, for-profit versus non-profit colleges, and alternative credentials, while also offering practical advice to guide prospective students and parents.

References

1. Jen Mishory, *The Future of Statewide College Promise Programs*, Century Foundation, n.d. *https://tcf.org/content/report/future-statewide-college-promise-programs/*
2. Robert Bozick, Drew M. Anderson and Lindsay Daugherty, "Patterns And Predictors Of Postsecondary Re-Enrollment In The Acquisition Of Stackable Credentials, *Social Science Research*, 98, August 2021. https://doi.org/10.1016/j.ssresearch.2021.102573

VIEWPOINT 1

> *"Community colleges are plugged into their local market: They're responsive to the employment and economic need of their local communities and region."*

The Benefits of Community College

Eileen Hoenigman Meyer

In this viewpoint, Eileen Hoenigman Meyer discusses some of the benefits of attending a community college through sharing the perspectives of community college staff and students. She argues that community colleges are more student-oriented than universities because they do not prioritize research over the student experience. They also are attuned to the unique characteristics and needs of the local community in a way that can better help students prepare for the workforce. Community colleges offer opportunities to students with life circumstances that make attending a university and completing a bachelor's program challenging or are looking for an affordable and efficient way to advance their careers. Eileen Hoenigman Meyer is a freelance writer focusing on topics such as job searching, work, family life, writing, and raising children.

"'Community College Saved Me': Honoring Community College Awareness Month," by Eileen Hoenigman Meyer, HigherEdJobs, April 28, 2021, https://www.higheredjobs.com/Articles/articleDisplay.cfm?ID=2681#:~:text=Not%20only%20do%20you%20save,do%20activities%20outside%20of%20academics.%22. Licensed under CC BY-ND 4.0 International.

Are There Suitable Alternatives to Traditional Higher Education?

As you read, consider the following questions:

1. According to this viewpoint, are community colleges able to award bachelor's degrees?
2. What impact did the COVID-19 pandemic have on community college enrollment?
3. What benefits of attending a community college does Genesis Gutierrez mention in this viewpoint?

April is Community College Awareness Month, and this year we have plenty of reasons to honor these important institutions. In addition to providing quality, affordable education to local students, community colleges are support and resource centers during times of crisis. These vital institutions have come through in a range of important ways during the pandemic.

The Association of Community College Trustees (ACCT) explains: "Community colleges throughout the country proved their worth to their communities over the past year, as they came to the aid of students as well as to their greater communities. For example, when the pandemic took the country by storm, community colleges immediately responded by accelerating education for nursing and other healthcare students, by lending dormitories to exhausted hospital workers for needed rest, by mass-producing masks and other personal protective equipment using fabrication facilities, and much more."

Another way in which community colleges have taken center stage this year: First Lady, Dr. Jill Biden, is a community college English professor. She taught for 15 years at Delaware Technical College, and she will continue her work at Northern Virginia Community College (NOVA), where she taught from 2009–2017 when she was Second Lady of the United States. She is the first FLOTUS in history to hold a paying job while serving as First Lady.

Dr. B, as her students and colleagues call her, remarked in comments she delivered at the 2015 Community College National Legislative Summit: "the responsibility for educating students is not the student's alone. It is a responsibility that belongs to all of us. Community colleges are uniquely positioned to fulfill this responsibility—to meet the needs of the actual community where they live—whether that means partnering with local employers on credentialing, working to make sure classes are flexible for working families, or supporting a seamless transition to a four-year degree. Because, we all reap the benefits when our citizens are well-educated and well-trained. It means that our economies are more vibrant, and our future is brighter."

Community colleges are important community resource centers that make education affordable and accessible. This April we honor these valuable institutions for higher learning.

The Lowdown on Community Colleges

According to Statista's Erin Duffy, as of 2020 there were 942 public community colleges across the US. Community colleges offer an affordable, streamlined approach to credentialing. While traditionally, these institutions offered two-year associate degrees, Mary Fulton, writing for the Education Commission of the States (ECS) points out that almost half of the states "allow community colleges to award bachelor's degrees as one strategy to meet workforce demands, increase access to educational and career advancement opportunities, address affordability and raise attainment rates."

This affordable credentialling can be especially helpful to adult learners. Kevin E. Drumm writes in *The New American College Town*: "As the nation's economy becomes increasingly specialized, as where one studies becomes less important than what one studies, and as the cost of earning a bachelor's degree continues to rise, the importance of community colleges to their communities should only grow. Further, community colleges are by, for, and of the community, so who better to drive economic initiatives."

Community colleges offer a good solution when it comes to affordable credentialing and upskilling. Surprisingly, though, community college enrollment has been down nationally during the pandemic. The National Student Clearinghouse Research Center reports: "A 13.1 percent drop in freshman enrollment (or over 327,500 students) from last fall is unprecedented. Sharp declines at public two-year institutions (over 207,200 students, 21% decrease) contributed the most to the decline, falling at a rate almost 20 times higher than the prior year's decline (pre-pandemic)."

A Community of Believers

Community colleges launch students into the workforce as well as into other academic programs. These institutions are an affordable way to experiment with different professional avenues to decide which one might be a fit.

Phil Ollenberg, assistant registrar at Bow Valley College shares: "Community colleges are plugged into their local market: They're responsive to the employment and economic need of their local communities and region. They're there to help get people employed and drive the local economy."

In his role, Ollenberg watches and discusses higher education trends in the US and Canada. He explains that he appreciates community colleges because, "They're focused on students, not on research projects/endowments: When I studied at and worked for a big university, I always felt like the students were second-fiddle to the research endowments and faculty research projects. Community colleges' core is in teaching and graduating students in responsive fields." Ollenberg also finds community college to be a good value for students. He explains: "They're generally excellent financial choices... with a closer focus on teaching and graduating students, their spending is more reigned-in leading to significantly lower tuition costs and a better investment by students and their families."

Genesis Gutierrez has experienced this firsthand as a community college student. She explains some of the lessons that community college students can garner: "You understand how to work with all kinds of people who come from all walks of life. . . . You understand the real-world before you even graduate from college, something I've learned is very hard for students who did not attend community college."

Gutierrez sees community college as "the smarter choice. Not only do you save a ton of money, it gives you more freedom to explore your career options wisely without feeling pressured. Once you hit a four-year university, you're pressured to pick a major and a career vs in community college you have time to explore your options and still do activities outside of academics."

"A Judgment-Free Zone"

Gutierrez points out that community college is where students go to better themselves and learn who they are and what they're capable of; the experience is both skill and esteem building.

Gutierrez explains: "What makes me so proud to be associated with community college is being surrounded by students who truly had to create their own unique path to whatever they chose to do with their degrees/careers. Students who just want to better themselves but may not have the means to or students who just need time to themselves to figure it all out. It's a judgment-free zone. You're truly just focused on you and your own needs."

"Community College Saved Me"

Gutierrez shares a success story that speaks to the true value of community colleges: "I graduated high school with a 2.8 GPA and over 100+ absences," she writes. "I had no idea what I wanted to do and was more than frustrated with my future. . . Community college saved me. I learned to care about my grades because of the incredible support system I had at the college (counselors, staff, coaches, teachers). . . I learned to love school and my future. Community college gave me the option to attend universities I would've never been able to go [to] straight out of high school. (I got into every school I applied to—UCLA, UCR, UCI, and UCSB). I believe it's an important message to share. . . There are truly other ways to get to your dream university."

Community colleges give students an affordable avenue to refine their skills, hone their talents, and pursue their dreams.

VIEWPOINT 2

> *"The fact that there have been concerns with the quality of feedback and higher education has been well-established in the literature"*

Factors Contributing to Low Success Rates for Community College Students

Amy Hankins and Christine Harrington

In this excerpted viewpoint, Amy Hankins and Christine Harrington point out that although community colleges in the U.S. have much to offer in terms of diversity, there are a significant number of such institutions where students, particularly students of color, failed to attain long-term education goals. These ongoing educational achievement gaps not only contribute to income inequality but are a disservice to students. One key factor for improvement is the quality of the learning experience, with effective feedback playing a key role in promoting good learning. Issues with providing effective feedback have been identified as timeliness, clarity, alignment with students' needs, and quantity of feedback, with students perceiving that they receive less feedback than instructors perceive themselves as providing. Amy Hankins is an associate professor of communications at Gateway Technical College, and Christine Harrington is a professor in the community college leadership doctoral program at Morgan State University.

"Lack of High-Quality, Frequent Feedback Contributes to Low Success Rates for Community College Students," by Amy Hankins and Christine Harrington, Impacting Education, November 17, 2022. https://impactinged.pitt.edu/ojs/ImpactingEd/article/view/201. Licensed under CC-BY-4.0 International

As you read, consider the following questions:

1. What are the main arguments presented in the viewpoint?
2. According to this viewpoint, do challenges associated with providing feedback in community colleges contribute to educational achievement gaps?
3. How can professors improve the feedback process for students?

Community colleges are open access, providing an educational path for people from all socioeconomic and educational backgrounds, and as a result, the student population is exceptionally diverse (Bailey et al., 2015). Unfortunately, most students who begin their education at a community college never reach their long-term educational goals. Fewer than four of every ten complete any type of degree or certificate within six years (Bailey et al., 2015). When the data are disaggregated, the completion rates are even lower for students of color. For instance, national statistics show that community colleges enroll 52 percent of all Black students and 57 percent of all Hispanic students in higher education (Baime & Baum, 2016), yet only 1 percent of Black students and 4 percent of Hispanic students graduate in two years (Complete College America, n.d.). This is problematic on so many levels. For one, educational achievement gaps of this magnitude point to a disparity of educational attainment for minorities in the United States. Persistent and increasing income inequity is a result of these achievement gaps (Hanushek et al., 2016). Unfortunately, Hanushek et al. (2016) found that the achievement gaps have remained essentially unchanged over almost half a century.

Although many factors contribute to student success, a significant factor is the learning experience. Achievement of the stated course learning outcomes and successful completion of the course is imperative for a student to move forward towards degree attainment. Seminal research from Adelman (2005, 2006) suggested that if a student does not successfully complete a course, their academic momentum is hindered. Furthermore, Adelman (2006) stated that his studies indicated students' excessive course withdrawal was "one of the most degree crippling features of undergraduate histories" (p. xxii) preventing students from finishing college.

Pedagogical practices have an undeniable impact on community college students' success. Feedback, in particular, has been shown to be a powerful educational tool, and if used correctly, it is one of the main predictors of student success. Seminal research conducted by Hattie et al. (2014) stated that effective feedback from an instructor could be "one of the most effective instructional strategies for improving student performance and closing achievement gaps" (p.17). Hattie and Timperley (2007) reported a synthesis of over 500 meta-analyses involving hundreds of thousands of studies and effect sizes and millions of students. Over 100 factors that might influence achievement were cited, including attributes of the schools, students, instructors, and curricula. The average effect size was 0.40 (achievement improved 40% of a standard deviation), but the effect size for feedback was 0.79, which, at about twice the average effect size, further supports the hypothesis that feedback ranks among the top influencers on student performance (Hattie & Timperley, 2007). Feedback is an important component of student learning; Hattie and Yates's findings in 2014 suggested that effective feedback can double the rate of learning. If used incorrectly, however, feedback can drastically harm students' motivation and success (Hattie & Yates, 2014).

Literature on feedback reflects significant concerns regarding the quality of feedback and the manner in which instructional feedback is provided to students. For instance, some of the identified issues in the literature included the timeliness of the feedback, the clarity of the feedback, and the lack of opportunities for students to work with feedback (Brooks et al., 2019; Hattie & Yates, 2014; Hounsell et al., 2008; Scott, 2005). For example, Hounsell et al. (2008) researched student perceptions of feedback.

The dataset was comprised of 782 completed student questionnaires and 23 group interviews with a total of 69 students (Hounsell et al., 2008); students' overall perceptions included that feedback had not helped improve their ways of learning or studying. Specific concerns identified in this study echo the aforementioned concerns: the variance in quantity, quality, and timeliness of the feedback (Hounsell et al., 2008).

Another established issue regarding feedback is that of a gap between students' perception of feedback when compared to the perceptions of their instructors. Hattie and Yates (2014) reported instructors "allege they dispense much helpful feedback to their students at relatively high levels and they claim they do so routinely" (p. 52); yet, students reported otherwise. In a classroom observation, researchers found the amount of feedback students received was, in fact, much less than the instructors said they provided (Hattie & Yates, 2014). These findings of a significant variance in students' and faculty's perceptions about feedback have been echoed in numerous other studies (Lizzio & Wilson, 2008; Mulliner & Tucker, 2017; Robinson et al., 2013). For instance, first-year students reported dissatisfaction with timeliness and the meaningfulness of feedback, yet faculty asserted they disseminated quality, timely, and constructive feedback (Robinson et al., 2013).

The fact that there have been concerns with the quality of feedback in higher education has been well-established in the literature (Mulliner and Tucker, 2017; Robinson et al., 2013; Scott, 2005). It is a complex issue, however, given the powerful outcomes effective feedback can have to either foster or hinder student success, it is judicious to suggest community college students need more opportunities to learn from quality feedback to aid in their success. There is a clear discord between what faculty believe was being provided and how students reported the learning opportunities from that feedback (Lizzio & Wilson, 2008; Mulliner & Tucker, 2017; Robinson et al., 2013).

[…]

Method

A comprehensive search approach was used to investigate why students have not been getting enough quality feedback consisted of gathering three different types of data. First, I gathered information via conversations with faculty. These conversations were conducted to gain an understanding of practitioner experiences, values, beliefs, and perspectives related to teaching and learning. Next, I reviewed peer-reviewed research found using the library databases. Finally, I explored gray literature that was accessible via public scholarship.

[…]

Results and Discussion

As a result of the literature research process, three major themes were revealed as major contributing factors related to issues surrounding the feedback students receive on their assignments. First, faculty in higher education, though experts in their own field, have not had training in pedagogical practices before they begin teaching (Beach et al., 2006; Eddy, 2010; Levin, 2006; Townsend & Twombly, 2007.) Therefore, they often begin their careers unaware of how to provide effective, quality feedback to support their students' learning. Second, even if community college faculty did receive training in how to give quality feedback, faculty reported not having enough time to provide feedback due to teaching loads and other institutional duties and expectations. Finally, studies (Hattie & Timperley, 2007; Martinez, 2019) suggested that students have a negative perception of feedback. Often, students have not perceived feedback as a positive opportunity for learning, and therefore, they have not frequently used the feedback to revise work (Ackerman & Gross, 2010;Fiock & Garcia, 2019; Mulliner & Tucker, 2017; Sambell, 2016).

[…]

Conclusion

Community colleges, as open-access colleges, are available as educational benefits to millions of non-traditional students regardless of their socioeconomic or academic background (Bailey et al., 2015; Mellow & Heelan, 2015). In fact, more than 40 percent of the community college student population are students of color (Mellow & Heelan, 2015). According to the Community College Research Center (2020), only 39% of those attending community college are walking away with degrees. One especially important way to support student learning and achievement is through effective feedback (Hattie et al., 2016).

Unfortunately, college students are not provided with frequent, productive feedback (Ackerman & Gross, 2010; Brooks et al. 2019; Hattie & Yates, 2014; Hounsell et al., 2008; Scott, 2005). Findings from this literature review indicated that there were three main reasons why college students are not provided with high-quality, regular feedback. First, faculty have not been trained on effective teaching strategies in general and on feedback strategies specifically (Eddy, 2010; Levin, 2006). Faculty are also incredibly stretched in terms of time, and feedback is an extremely time-consuming task (Martinez, 2019; Morest, 2015). Finally, faculty get discouraged when students' perceptions of feedback are negative, and when students do not read and use the feedback provided to improve their work and learning (Cohan, 2020; Stern & Solomon, 2006).

To address the lack of training, colleges can provide professional development that specifically focuses on why feedback is a powerful learning tool and how to use it in the classroom to support their students' learning and success. For example, colleges could consider having a faculty learning community (FLC) to allow faculty an opportunity to learn effective feedback practices—like the importance of implementing scheduled opportunities for their students to engage with formative feedback (Brooks et al., 2019). Through initiatives like feedback-focused faculty learning communities, faculty can also learn how to incorporate opportunities within assignments for students to read feedback, make revisions as needed, and resubmit work.

Time was identified as barrier to faculty providing meaningful feedback to students. Thus, one approach can be to assist faculty with developing more time-efficient feedback strategies. For instance, encouraging faculty to use class time for this purpose or to provide targeted, formative feedback throughout the semester (Harrington, 2022). Offering training programs during already scheduled department, division, or college-wide meeting times is another way to address the time barrier (Harrington, 2020).

The final barrier of student perception can also be a challenge (Ackerman & Gross, 2010; Fiock & Garcia, 2019; Mulliner & Tucker, 2017; Sambell, 2016). Through faculty development, faculty can learn ways to better communicate the importance of feedback to their students. In essence, students need to understand why feedback is a positive and productive part of learning. "For feedback processes to be enhanced, students need both appreciation of how feedback can operate effectively and opportunities to use feedback within the curriculum" (Carless & Boud, 2018, p. 1315). Carless and Boud (2018) refer to this as feedback literacy, and they assert the importance of communicating feedback literacy to students early in the course, so students are mentally prepared for feedback. Explaining why feedback is powerful, what kind of feedback they can expect, and giving students clear expectations about the formative feedback loop are essential in setting the stage for more positive student interactions with the feedback (Carless & Boud, 2018; Gonzalez, 2020; Hattie & Timperley, 2007). Based on these findings, professional development for faculty is clearly needed. Innovative professional development programs where community college instructors can learn about the characteristics of effective feedback, be taught time-efficient strategies to provide feedback, and learn how to provide feedback in a manner that students will be more likely to act upon is essential. Community colleges that want to support student success can invest in teaching and learning centers and offer professional development on effective feedback practices. Students need and deserve frequent, high-quality feedback (Taras, 2006).

References

Ackerman, D., & Gross, B. (2010). Instructor feedback: How much do students really want? *Journal of Marketing Education*, 32(2), 172–181. https://doi.org/10.1177/0273475309360159

Adelman, C. (2005). *Moving into town—and moving on: The community college in the lives of traditional-age students.* U.S. Department of Education.https://www2.ed.gov/rschstat/research/pubs/comcollege/index.html

Adelman, C. (2006). *The toolbox revisited: Paths to degree completion from high school through college.* U.S. Department of Education. https://www2.ed.gov/rschstat/research/pubs/toolboxrevisit/toolbox.pdf

Bailey, T., Jaggars, S. S., & Jenkins, D. (2015). *Redesigning America's community colleges: A clearer path to student success.* Harvard University Press.

Baime, D., & Baum, S. (2016*). Community colleges: Multiple missions, diverse student bodies, and a range of policy solutions.* Urban Institute.

Beach, A., Sorcinelli, M.D., Austin, A., & Rivard, J. (2016). *Faculty development in the age of evidence.* Stylus Publishing.

Bickerstaff, S., & Chavarín, O. (2018). Understanding the needs of part-time faculty at six community colleges. CCRC Research Brief. *Community College Research Center.* https://ccrc.tc.columbia.edu/media/k2/attachments/understanding-part-time-faculty-community-colleges.pdf

Brooks, C., Carroll, A., Gillies, R. M., & Hattie, J. (2019). A matrix of feedback for learning. *Australian Journal of Teacher Education*, 44(4), https://doi.org/10.14221/ajte.2018v44n4.2

Carless, D. & Boud, D. (2018). The development of student feedback literacy: Enabling uptake of feedback. *Assessment & Evaluation in Higher Education*, 43(8), 1315–1325, https://doi.org/10.1080/02602938.2018.1463354

Cohan, D. (2020). How to grade faster in 2020. *Inside Higher Ed.* https://www.insidehighered.com/advice/2020/02/11/advice-grading-more-efficiently-option Community College Research Center. (2020). *Community college FAQs.*https://ccrc.tc.columbia.edu/Community-College-FAQs.html

Complete College America. (n.d.) *Data dashboard.* https://completecollege.org/data-dashboard/

Cox, R. (2010). *The college fear factor: How students and professors misunderstand one another.* Harvard University Press.

Eddy, P. (2010). *Community college leadership: A multidimensional model for leading* (1sted.) Stylus Publishing.

Fiock, H., & Garcia, H. (2019). How to give your students better feedback with technology. *The Chronicle of Higher Education.* https://www.chronicle.com/interactives/20191108-Advice-Feedback

Frey, N., Fisher, D., & Hattie, J. (2018). Developing "assessment capable" learners: If we want students to take charge of their learning, we can't keep relegating them to a passive role in the assessment process. *Educational Leadership*,75(5), 46–51.

Gonzalez, J. (Host). (2018, January). Moving from feedback to feedforward (No.87) [Audio podcast episode]. *Cult of Pedagogy.* https://www.cultofpedagogy.com/feedforward/

Hanushek, E., Peterson, P., Talpey, L., & Woessmann, L. (2016). The achievement gap fails to close. *Education Next,* 19(3), 8–17. https://www.educationnext.org/achievement-gap-fails-close-half-century-testing-shows-persistent-divide/

Harrington, C. (2020). *Ensuring learning: Supporting faculty to improve student success.* American Association of Community Colleges and Rowman and Littlefield.

Harrington, C. (2022). *Keeping us engaged: Student perspectives (and research-based strategies) on what works and why.* Stylus.

Hattie, J., Fisher, D., & Frey, N. (2016). Do they hear you? *Educational Leadership*, 73(7), 16–21.

Hattie, J., & Timperley, H. (2007). The power of feedback. *Review of Educational Research*, 77(1), 81–112. https://doi.org/10.3102/003465430298487Hattie, J., & Yates, G. (2014). Using feedback to promote learning. In V. A. Benassi, C.E. Overson, & C.M. Hakala (Eds.), *Applying science of learning in education: Infusing psychological science into the curriculum* (pp. 45-58). Society for the Teaching of Psychology. http://teachpsych.org/ebooks/asle2014/index.php

Hounsell, D., McCune, V., Hounsell, J., & Litjens, J. (2008). The quality of guidance and feedback to students. *Higher Education Research and Development*, 27(1),55–67. https://doi.org/10.1080/07294360701658765

Jonsson, A. (2012). Facilitating productive use of feedback in higher education. *Active Learning in Higher Education*, 14(1),63–76. sagepub.co.uk/journalsPermissions.nav. https://doi.org/10.1177/1469787412467125

Levin, A. (2006). *Educating school teachers.* The Education Schools Project.

Lizzio, A. & Wilson, K. (2008). Feedback on assessment: Students' perceptions of quality and effectiveness. *Assessment & Evaluation in Higher Education*, 33(3), 263–275. https://doi.org/10.1080/026029307012

Mallett, R., Hagen-Zanker, J., Slater, R. & Duvendack, M. (2012). The benefits and challenges of using systematic reviews in international development research. *Journal of Development Effectiveness*, 4(3), 445–455, https://doi.org/10.1080/19439342.2012.711342

Martinez, E. (2019). The rules change: Exploring faculty experiences and work expectations within a drifting community college context. *Community College Review*, 47(2), 111–135. https://doi.org//10.1177/0091552119835022

Mellow, G. O., & Heelan, C. M. (2015). *Minding the dream: The process and practice of the American community college* (2nded.). Rowman & Littlefield.

Molloy, E., & Boud, D. (2013). *Feedback in higher and professional education: Understanding it and doing it well.* Routledge.

Morest, V. S. (2015). Faculty scholarship at community colleges: Culture, institutional structures, and socialization. *New Directions for Community Colleges*, 171, 21–36.

Mulliner, E., & Tucker, M. (2017). Feedback on feedback practice: Perceptions of students and academics. *Assessment & Evaluation in Higher Education*, 42(2), 266–288. https://doi.org//10.1080/02602938.2015.1103365

National Study of Postsecondary Faculty.(2005). *2004 national study of postsecondary faculty (NSOPF: 04): Report on faculty and instructional staff in fall 2003*. National Center for Education Statistics. https://nces.ed.gov/pubs2005/2005172.pdf

Petticrew, M., & Roberts, H. (2006). *Systematic reviews in the social sciences: A practical guide*. Blackwell. https://doi.org/10.1002/9780470754887

Robinson, S., Pope, D. & Holyoak, L. (2013). Can we meet their expectations? Experiences and perceptions of feedback in first year undergraduate students. *Assessment & Evaluation in Higher Education*, 38(3), 260–272. https://doi.org/10.1080/02602938.2011.629291

Sambell, K. (2016). Assessment and feedback in higher education: Considerable room for improvement? *Student Engagement in Higher Education*, 1(1), 1–14. http://insight.cumbria.ac.uk/id/eprint/2819

Sallee, M. W . (2008). Work and family balance: How community college faculty cope. *New Directions for Community Colleges*,2008(142), 81–91. https://doi.org/10.1002/cc.327

Scott, G. (2005). *Accessing the student voice*. Department of Education, Science and Training.

Stern, L. & Solomon, A. (2006). Effective faculty feedback: The road less traveled. *Assessing Writing, 11*(2006), 22–41. https://doi.org/10.1016/j.asw.2005.12.001

Taras, M. (2006). Do unto others or not: Equity in feedback for undergraduates. *Assessment & Evaluation in Higher Education*, 31(3), 365–377.

Taylor, S. S. (2011). I really don't know what he meant by that: How well do engineering students understand teachers' comments on their writing? *Technical Communication Quarterly*, 20(2), 139–166. https://doi.org/10.1080/10572252.2011.548762

Townsend, B. K., & Twombly, S. B. (2007). Community college faculty: Overlooked and undervalued. *ASHE Higher Education Report*, 32(6), 1–163.

Warner, J. (2017). The 'administrative fiction' of faculty workloads. *Inside Higher Ed*. https://www.insidehighered.com/blogs/just-visiting/administrative-fiction-faculty-workloads

Wiggins, G. (2012). Seven keys to effective feedback. *Educational Leadership, 70*(1), 10–16.

Viewpoint 3

> *"The path to a bachelor's degree looks less formidable when a student can earn a certificate of accomplishment in a semester or less."*

Can Stackable Credentials Offer an Alternative to a College Degree?
Robert A. Scott

In this viewpoint, Robert A. Scott asserts that in an era when it has become increasingly unlikely for students to enroll in bachelor's degree programs due to the cost of these programs and the job opportunities available, stackable credentials have become a more attractive option to many students. This offers educational opportunities to students who have completed some college but did not receive a degree as well as people who are seeking paths to professional advancement. Scott argues that it would benefit universities to offer more stackable credentials in order to stay on top of current trends in higher education. Robert A. Scott is President Emeritus and University Professor Emeritus of Adelphi University.

"Stackable Credentials: Building Enrollment Growth Through Program Design," by Robert A. Scott, HigherEdJobs, May 18, 2023, https://www.higheredjobs.com/Articles/articleDisplay.cfm?ID=3447&Title=Stackable%20Credentials%3A%20Building%20Enrollment%20Growth%20Through%20Program%20Design/. Licensed under CC BY-ND 4.0 International.

Are There Suitable Alternatives to Traditional Higher Education?

As you read, consider the following questions:

1. According to statistics cited in this viewpoint, what percent of students who start pursuing a bachelor's degree drop out after their first year?
2. How does Scott define stacked credentials in this viewpoint?
3. What are some careers and industries that are particularly suited to stackable credentials, according to Scott?

College enrollments are a grave concern to campus leaders. There are nearly 1 million fewer students since before the pandemic began. Undergraduate enrollment alone dropped 466,000 students, or 3.1%.

When we add in the projected decline in high school graduates, the changes in college-going behavior due to costs and job opportunities, and the drop in international student recruitment, we can see why colleges and universities are seeking new ways to meet enrollment goals. The first step is to improve year-to-year retention. Nearly one-quarter of those who start a bachelor's degree program drop out after one year. The second step is to improve graduation rates. About one-third of four-year college students fail to graduate in six years.

Next, more campuses are developing pathways to re-enrollment for those with some college credits but no degree. There are nearly 39 million people in this condition. Still, other institutions are developing so-called "stackable" programs.

The goals of stackable programs such as the Career Launchpad at Metropolitan State University of Denver are to improve access for students who aren't certain about attending college and provide periodic milestones of achievement. Such milestones not only motivate students with shorter paths to a credential but also provide an exit point with evidence of accomplishment for employers. The idea is to recognize the accomplishment of specialized expertise, as well as general knowledge, that employers value. Such programs are classic "win-win-win" for students, colleges, and employers.

Stacked credentials are individual achievements accumulated over time. These periodic certifications and credentials are called "stackable" because they can be designed to "stack" on top of each other, thus building to something more substantial. This model is also called a "career ladder," with each rung on the ladder representing a step up in professional accomplishment. These are recognizable awards, evidence of skills and abilities learned and practiced. As microcredentials, they can be accomplished in short chunks of time.

The path to a bachelor's degree looks less formidable when a student can earn a certificate of accomplishment in a semester or less. Think of merit badges in Scouts: each recognizes a milestone but many are required for the top reward of Eagle Scout or Gold

What Are Stackable Credentials?

Stackable credentials don't require students to enroll in a program in college and allow them to take courses on their own time. Stackable credentials are an excellent option for students who can't take on a full course load for a variety of reasons. Students will be able to complete courses in a shorter amount of time and can take as many classes as they want to. You can stack these courses to complete prerequisites for other courses to then create a degree or certificate. This type of stacking is vertical stacking. Students can also receive a variety of credentials from classes that are at the same level which is horizontal stacking. This is a great option for students who want to refresh their education on some courses for their careers.

Why Do Students Get Stackable Credentials?

Students choose stackable credentials for a variety of reasons. Some students want to advance in their careers but don't want to go back to school full-time. They can take these quick courses to sharpen their skills to get a pay raise or promotion at work. For

Award. The premise is that students will gain confidence with each achievement and thus be motivated to take the next step. But if they must stop out for family or financial reasons, they will have earned a job-related, employer-recognized credential to show for their effort.

Ideally, these career ladder programs are designed with industry or professional association, or union, assistance to ensure labor market value. They also require regular advising by instructors. The credentials can then be acknowledged as ascending benchmarks, demonstrated skills, and competencies.

The most common career ladder approaches are in education and nursing, but the model can be applied in many other fields with some innovative thinking. In education, the "stackable" option is Teacher Certification as a companion to a degree in another subject, usually a liberal arts major.

> others, stackable credentials allow them to focus on one or two classes at a time so they can study harder and do better in those classes. Not everyone learns at the same pace, so students can take their time to build the degree they want when they don't have to take a full course load.
>
> ### How Do Stackable Credentials Work?
>
> Students can horizontally or vertically stack their credentials. For vertical stacking, you use classes to advance to the next level of courses and eventually build an entire degree or enough classes for a certificate. For horizontal stacking, you take a variety of courses on the same level that help you learn more about certain subjects. Horizontally stacked courses are a great option for those who are looking to advance their career because you are going into more detail in only one or two subjects. Stackable credentials allow students to build their knowledge, degree, and certifications without having to commit to getting a full degree at once.
>
> "Stackable Credentials: A New College Trend," College Raptor, December 21, 2022.

Nursing has several levels of licensure, including LPN (Licensed Practical Nurse), Associate of Science RN (Registered Nurse), and BSN (Bachelor of Science in Nursing). Therefore, students can progress from LPN to an associate degree to a bachelor's degree through continuous learning, on and off-ramps, and licensed certifications at each stage. In addition to professional education, candidates have required courses in general education to ensure an introduction to the liberal arts as well as sciences.

A similar career ladder model is used in other fields, including information technology, engineering, and business. Microsoft has four levels of Excel certifications. Such certificates can be used to fill in skills gaps, helping the candidate qualify for a job, a promotion, or a raise.

Stackable credentials can be designed to be vertical, i.e., rising in difficulty and complexity; horizontal, i.e., combining related topics in a package; and hybrid, i.e., a combination of vertical and horizontal stacking.

Nearly one in ten undergraduates is working toward a stackable certificate, according to the Georgetown Center on Education and the Workforce. Major providers include online course companies like Western Governors University and edX as well as institutions such as Metropolitan State University of Denver.

Colleges and universities must be innovative if they are to be sustainable. Renewed attention to recruitment, retention, reengagement, and program design are essential, and stackable credentials are one means to combine all four approaches.

VIEWPOINT 4

> *"Proprietary education providers can innovate more like the private sector. We can quickly identify and react to changing student and workplace needs, developing programs that provide the knowledge and skills students require."*

Are Online Learning and For-Profit Colleges the Future of Higher Education?

Gary E. McCullough and Andrew Hibel

In this viewpoint, Gary E. McCullough and Andrew Hibel discuss two alternatives to traditional non-profit institutions of higher education: online education and for-profit education (sometimes known as proprietary education). McCullough points out that online education plays an important role in providing educational opportunities to people who cannot afford to quit their jobs and return to school full-time. This viewpoint was published in 2010—well before the COVID-19 pandemic made online education popular—but even at that time it was helping make higher education more attainable. For-profit colleges also offer greater flexibility for students unable to attend full-time and have the added advantage of being able to quickly institute new programs in response to current trends. Gary E. McCullough is President and CEO of Career Education Corporation, and Andrew Hibel is the Chief Operating Officer and Co-Founder of HigherEdJobs.

"Online Learning and the World of For Profit Education," by Gary E. McCullough and Andrew Hibel, HigherEdJobs, September 20, 2010, https://www.higheredjobs.com/HigherEdCareers/interviews.cfm?ID=224. Licensed under CC BY-ND 4.0 International.

The Future of Higher Education

As you read, consider the following questions:

1. What does McCullough say is the difference between online and distance learning?
3. According to McCullough, what is the focus of faculty at for-profit (proprietary) schools? How does this focus differ from that of traditional non-profit schools?
2. What statistic does McCullough cite from a 2009 study by the Department of Education about online learning?

Is online learning the wave of the future? How are proprietary institutions different than traditional universities? What is all the recent press regarding for-profit institutions? The answers to these questions, the addressing of misconceptions and much more are discussed in this month's conversation with Gary E. McCullough, the President and CEO of Career Education Corporation. The colleges, schools and universities that are part of the Career Education Corporation offer education to over 116,000 students across the world in a variety of career-oriented disciplines. We examine the aspects of online education and for-profit education and how it affects students, faculty and administrators in today's market.

Andrew Hibel, HigherEdJobs: Mr. McCullough, you are currently the President and CEO of Career Education Corporation. Prior to joining the company, you served in leadership roles in traditional Fortune 500 companies. What prompted you to make the switch to the world of higher education?

Gary E. McCullough, Career Education Corporation: When I was first approached about the CEO position at Career Education Corporation, I was skeptical about proprietary education. So I did some homework, which included my own "mystery shopping" of schools. I posed as a parent of a prospective student and had a very positive experience. That convinced me to leave the security of what I was doing and join Career Education. I appreciate the challenge of helping our company evolve as a true leader in postsecondary education. Most importantly, it's tremendously rewarding to see how we're changing lives through education.

Hibel: As mentioned in Career Education Corporation's background statement on your website, over 40% of your students attend web-based virtual campuses. Why do you think it is so important to offer this option to students?

McCullough: It's a challenging economy and most adults recognize the need to stay current, whether their field is accounting, information technology, health care, business or education. Today, for many people it is simply not an option to take a leave of absence or quit a job to complete a degree. People have commitments, whether at work or at home caring for children or other family members.

Online education provides busy people the convenience and flexibility of a 24/7 platform for learning. The majority of our students are working adults over 30 who have returned to school to get a degree to help advance or change their careers. They appreciate the opportunity to receive an education while balancing family and work. It is our responsibility to meet their needs by delivering high-quality education.

Hibel: According to a Distance Education and Training Council (DETC) survey, sponsored by the DETC (a distance education accreditation body), 95% of students attending a distance program reported they achieved their learning goals; 97% were satisfied overall with their studies; and 97% reported that they would recommend their alma mater to someone else to enroll. What are your thoughts on these impressive statistics?

McCullough: These are impressive statistics, certainly. It's important to remember the distinction between online education and distance education. With both approaches, learning is conducted off-site. However, distance education may include correspondence studies, audio/visual material and local tutorials, as well as web-based content. Online education delivers course content using web-based technologies exclusively. For example, courses at the online campuses of American InterContinental University and Colorado Technical University use sophisticated, award-winning web technology that puts everything a student needs for study at his or her fingertips. We're constantly looking for ways to innovate, using technology to meet students' varying needs for learning.

Hibel: In the book, *Online Learning Today: Strategies That Work*, the author states "E-learning isn't the next big thing—it's the NOW big thing." Do you think that the higher education community, both non-profit and for-profit, can agree with this concept?

McCullough: Absolutely. A 2009 study from the Department of Education concluded that students who took all or part of their classes online performed better, on average, than those taking the same course through traditional face-to-face instruction. Students today demand options to fit their busy schedules and online learning offers the flexibility needed to attract and retain those students. More and more courses are delivered entirely or partially online. This is driven by student preferences for flexibility. And it's clearly effective.

More traditional institutions are beginning to offer online programs, but proprietary institutions like ours have led the way. We invest in new technology, innovate rapidly and have the ability to quickly shift programs based on student demand and preferences.

In 2010, Colorado Technical University introduced My Unique Student Experience (M.U.S.E.™) as part of its virtual campus. M.U.S.E. offers "freedom learning" for students, who can select from 11 different ways to interact with course material. Students pick the format that best suits their learning style. Among the choices, students can watch videos, read materials, listen to instructors, solve problems, take practice tests or explore related topics.

Hibel: Enrollment in online classes at universities has grown 20 percent annually over the last five years according to Bruce Chaloux, director of student access programs and services and the electronic campus for the Southern Regional Education Board in Texas. Despite this gain in enrollment numbers, there are still some challenges with online degrees, such as the perception by some people that they are of limited quality. What would you say in response to this?

McCullough: I think that perception continues to change. Evidence of student and employer acceptance of the value of online education is found in the growth statistics, as cited by Chaloux. While proprietary colleges and universities are at the forefront of online education, traditional four-year and community colleges are ramping up to include hybrid and all-online learning.

Why are the non-profit schools following our lead? First, we are a highly mobile, global community of adult learners who demand a flexible 24/7 platform that meets our learning goals and lifestyles. Second, high school students today and those who will follow are growing up online with virtual campuses, virtual classrooms and web communities. There is no going back. Online education has the power to transform the landscape of education. It's not an evolution, it's a revolution.

Hibel: In a book titled, *New Players, Different Game*, the authors present the for-profit model as "changing the rules of the game," in regards to how higher education models operate. Would you briefly outline some of the major differences in how for-profit models work versus a traditional non-profit university?

McCullough: Let's first establish that we have one element in common—whether governed by a board of directors or board of trustees, students are always our top priority. Our collective mission is to ensure students receive the best education possible so that they can build meaningful careers, raise the quality of their lives, and help to stimulate the overall economy.

The rise in proprietary education occurred because an increased demand for higher education programs and degrees could not be met by traditional colleges and universities. The demand is market-driven. Employers need qualified employees to fill positions critical to economic growth. Employees want to remain current in their field and relevant to their employers. So our education institutions are market-driven in ways that benefit both students and employers. We know we've been successful when a student completes a program of study and finds employment, whether a new job or promotion, in his or her chosen field.

In this environment, we must be flexible and in step with the market—which drives innovation. Unlike traditional university bureaucracies, which are reliant on donors, alumni and state budget funds, proprietary institutions are more agile and can quickly invest in new programs as the demands of the job market change. We can scale up and down easily, while maintaining convenient course schedules and fostering new program development in the best interests of our students.

Even with exciting new technologies, faculty members remain the most important student-facing resource we have. But unlike at many traditional non-profit schools, teaching is the primary function of our faculty. Rather than investing in research, proprietary institutions like CEC invest in faculty development and resources for students.

Where non-profit universities are geared to full-time traditional students, we typically serve adult learners who require flexibility. There are no semesters or trimesters, and classes are scheduled year-round at times that are convenient for students busy juggling work and family responsibilities.

Proprietary institutions are often criticized for having profit motives. The fact is we're innovating to meet the needs of today's students. If we don't deliver for our students, we fail. Only by keeping a keen focus on student success do we succeed as a business. Again, it's all about changing lives through education.

Hibel: What do you see some of the major challenges as well as the major advantages that for-profit universities and colleges have compared to their traditional non-profit university counterparts?

McCullough: Non-profit universities are generally places filled with tradition. Having graduated from two non-profit universities, I appreciate the storied environment on campus. But for all they offer, those institutions can be slow to change. A large bureaucracy often requires many levels of review and approvals before program change can be made.

We're different. Proprietary education providers can innovate more like the private sector. We can quickly identify and react to changing student and workplace needs, developing programs that provide the knowledge and skills students require.

So it should come as no surprise that private sector education companies like ours have led the way in developing online education tools that are transforming the way people learn now and into the future. Our focus on meeting student demands without undue constraints gives us the freedom to develop new educational programs now.

Hibel: The Post-9/11 Veterans Educational Assistance Act of 2008 (Chapter 33), which went into effect August 1, 2009, enables delivery of new tuition, fees, and housing allowance benefits to eligible veterans. Have you seen any changes in military personnel taking advantage of the opportunity to further their education with these benefits? If so, why do you think this is occurring?

McCullough: As a former U.S. Army officer, I'm proud of the commitment our nation is making today educating our active military and veterans. The sacrifices our soldiers and their families are making today in places like Afghanistan are worthy of our reinvestment in them.

The intent of this new bill is to recognize the contributions of active military personnel and veterans serving on or after Sept. 11, 2001, and we have seen a number of changes since the bill's passage in 2009.

The Post-9/11 GI Bill improves upon the WWII-era GI bill. It increases funding for tuition and fees, extends the benefit period from 10 to 15 years and offers the option of transferring the education benefit to a spouse or child.

For the first time, veterans may attend their institution of choice, where "choice" is not wholly dependent on tuition rates. Prior to passage of the new bill, veterans and military students had to balance what they wanted in an education with what they could afford with the benefit pay-out. All too often a student's first consideration was the cost of tuition and not school selection or the particular degree program.

Under the Post 9/11 GI Bill, eligible veterans may receive education benefits based on the cost of tuition and fees at the most expensive in-state undergraduate institution of higher education in the state in which he or she is enrolled. A monthly housing allowance of about $1,400 per month also puts many veterans in a better position to complete their education. They can devote their time and energy to their studies, with less concern about making ends meet.

We're also seeing parents use the opportunity to contribute to the education of their spouse or child through an education benefit transfer option. This is particularly important to military service members at the end of their careers with little interest in continuing their own education. Our staff meets frequently with parents at base education fairs to discuss degree and program options and outcomes for their children. My team finds working with military parents and their children extremely rewarding and believes the Post-9/11 GI Bill has been of great help to those who have served our country.

Hibel: Proposed changes in regulation of for-profit institutions have been hot topics in the news lately. What are your thoughts on the recent press?

McCullough: There certainly has been a lot of press coverage on the proposed changes. We're hopeful the result will be a fair and balanced approach to ensuring equal access to education for traditionally underserved ethnically and culturally diverse student populations.

Unfortunately, some of the proposed regulations—particularly one commonly referred to as "gainful employment"—would have the unintended consequences of limiting educational access so important to our students. The proposed rule would not be applied even-handedly across all of higher education, instead employing complicated and discriminatory debt-to-income ratios and student loan repayment rates targeted at private-sector institutions. These metrics are not in the best interests of students because they would force many quality programs to close. By impeding students' access to and choice of quality programs currently available, the "gainful employment" rule threatens to undermine President Obama's goal of 8 million more college graduates by 2020.

It's interesting to note that if applied to non-profit schools, more than 500 traditional colleges or universities would fail the Department of Education's "gainful employment" test.

We hope that sensible heads prevail on this issue.

Hibel: There are numerous opportunities today for instructors to teach online or through "e-learning" capabilities. What would your suggestions be to a potential faculty member who is looking to make the transition from a traditional on-campus teaching position to a position that is taught using distance education technology?

McCullough: The key to effective teaching, whether it is in a physical classroom or in a virtual classroom, is student engagement. As I mentioned, CEC's course delivery system, M.U.S.E., allows students to engage with the content in a variety of ways, depending upon their learning style. Our online faculty is trained to establish student expectations about learning online, to be responsive to student inquiry, to provide timely and constructive feedback and to facilitate interaction among students.

My guidance to anyone interested in teaching online would be the same guidance I would provide to anyone interested in enrolling in online courses—it is not easier online. In fact, it may be more challenging. While online learning affords us the ability to be flexible as to when and where educational interaction occurs between students, faculty, peers and the content, the amount of time and level of effort are by no means diminished.

Hibel: In the book, *For-Profit Colleges and Universities*, it was suggested that "just as a desire for academic freedom determined how faculty work was constructed at traditional institutions, the curriculum determines academic work at proprietary institutions." What is your response to this in regards to a potential faculty member who may be interested in working in a for-profit college or university?

McCullough: Faculty employed by traditional institutions of higher education have three responsibilities: research, service to the institution through participation in governance and teaching. This contrasts with the singular focus of the faculty member at proprietary institutions of higher education, which is to facilitate student learning.

Typically, proprietary institutions of higher education employ practitioners who are subject-matter experts with the appropriate credentials to teach. This provides students the opportunity to engage with experts who not only know their content, but who are personally familiar with the application of the content in the workplace. Learners are better able to understand concepts when the relevancy is made clear through examples of how it's applied in the workplace. Practitioners as educators are able to contextualize their knowledge and share perspective. To me, that's academic freedom.

As for curriculum, ours is developed by our subject matter experts—our faculty. We begin by identifying students' desired career outcomes and then engage employers and consult industry standards to determine the knowledge, skills and competencies students need to develop through their program of study. To say the "curriculum determines the academic work at proprietary institutions" is not accurate. In fact, our faculty determine and continually revise the appropriate curricula.

Hibel: For someone looking to start a career as an administrator in higher education, specifically, at a for-profit institution, what is your advice to them?

McCullough: A career in higher education administration requires the candidate be ready, willing and able to serve a diverse student population and put the interests of students first. As a campus leader, you are the face and external voice of the institution at all times. And, whether you are a department chair, finance director or school president, you must be knowledgeable about governing practices and accrediting bodies. You must be prepared to engage in a process of continuous improvement that includes data collection, analysis, development of strategic plans, as well as evaluation of the impact of those plans. These are the minimum requirements of any administrative position.

In proprietary post-secondary education, we look for candidates who are flexible, creative, thrive on innovation, and are willing to quickly change direction to meet the needs of our students.

The Future of Higher Education

Periodical and Internet Sources Bibliography

The following articles have been selected to supplement the diverse views presented in this chapter.

Luis Armona, Rajashri Chakrabarti, and Michael F. Lovenheim, "Student Debt and Default: The Role of For-Profit Colleges," *Journal of Financial Economics*, April 2022. https://doi.org/10.1016/j.jfienco/2021.12.008.

David Deming, Claudia Goldin, and Lawrence Katz, "For-Profit Colleges," *The Future of Children*, Spring 2013. https://www.jstor.org/stable/23409492.

David Leonhardt, "The College Access Index Return: A New Look At Economic Diversity In Higher Education," *New York Times*, September 8, 2023. https://www.nytimes.com/2023/09/08/briefing/college-access-low-income.html

Jack Mountjoy, "Community Colleges and Upward Mobility," *American Economic Review*, April 2022. https://doi.org/10.1016/j.jfineco.2021.12.008.

Elissa Nadworny, "Feds Offer Students New Protections Against Programs that Lead to High Debt, Low Pay," NPR, September 28, 2023. https://www.npr.org/2023/09/28/1202291883/for-profit-colleges-student-loans-affordable.

Don Olcott Jr., "Micro-Credentials: A Catalyst for Strategic Reset and Change in U.S. Higher Education," *American Journal of Distance Education*, December 2, 2021. https://www.tandfonline.com/doi/abs/10.1080/08923647.2021.1997537.

Chris Quintana, "Are For-Profit Colleges Worth the Cost? Graduates Are Split on the Value of Their Degrees," USA Today, January 31, 2023. https://www.usatoday.com/story/news/education/2023/01/31/for-profit-college-education-student-loan-debt/11136095002/.

Dileep Rao, "Higher Ed at a Crossroads: Multiple Impacts of AI and Marshall McLuhan," *Forbes*, October 5, 2023. https://www.forbes.com/sites/dileeprao/2023/10/05/higher-ed-at-a-crossroads-multiple-impacts-of-ai-and-marshall-mcluhan/?sh=76ad37e7e2ab.

Stephanie Riegg Cellini and Nicholas Turner, "Gainfully Employed?: Assessing The Employment And Earnings of For-Profit College Students Using Administrative Data," *Journal of Human Resources,* March 31, 2019. https://doi.org/10.3368/jhr.54.2.1016.8302R1.

Hilary Tackie, "Americans Have Mixed Feelings About Online Learning," New America, October 3, 2023. https://www.newamerica.org/education-policy/edcentral/americans-have-mixed-feelings-about-online-learning/.

CHAPTER 3

Can Higher Education Help Address Social Issues?

Chapter Preface

Universities educate, but their role in the United States has historically encompassed more than simply degree granting. In addition to giving students opportunities to gain knowledge, universities also develop students' critical thinking and analytical skills, providing the tools for lifelong learning, and preparing students to function as involved citizens in a democracy. These less tangible but important qualities of a university education have become subjects of increasing debate. While many believe that universities should educate students in the principles of democracy, civic engagement and social and professional responsibility, many others believe that universities should only focus on career preparation rather than issues around students' values and beliefs.

Here, progressive and conservative perspectives differ. The liberal perspective posits that students should become informed citizens and be exposed to different viewpoints while learning about civic engagement and social responsibility. The conservative perspective is that universities should not impose a liberal point of view about societal issues and should let students form and exercise their own opinions. The division between these two perspectives has deepened recently, leading to heated debates about the structure, funding and staffing of universities while disagreeing over the values, beliefs, and practices of higher education institutions.[1]

The impact on colleges and universities is still emerging. Recently, for example, the governor of Florida targeted parts of the curricula deemed too political and prohibited public institutions of higher education from using state funding for Diversity, Equity, and Inclusion (DEI) programs[2]. Other states have started adopting similar legislation in order to influence what is taught in the classroom, both at the university level and in public primary and secondary schools. While these issues are still playing out, this chapter considers both conservative and liberal perspectives on these important issues.

The Future of Higher Education

The question of whether students at U.S. universities can be well or even fully educated without understanding issues of democracy, good citizenship, social responsibility, historical racism, and inequality remains under discussion. In addition, the issue of what is needed for students to effectively function in an interconnected world in which technology increasingly connects people across cultures and demographics remains pressing. The viewpoints in this chapter present opposing perspectives on higher education's role in an equitable society, guiding readers in a nuanced consideration of the issues, challenges and opportunities around participation in democracy, good citizenship, and effectiveness in a global world.

References

1. Jonathan Zimmerman, *Whose America? Culture Wars in The Public Schools*, 2022. Chicago, IL: University of Chicago Press.

2. Jocelyn Gecker, "Desantis' War on 'Woke' Colleges Sparks Fear Among Professors, Students," PBS Newshour, March 30, 2023. https://www.pbs.org/newshour/education/desantis-war-on-woke-colleges-sparks-fear-among-professors-students#:~:text=31%20aimed%20at%20overhauling%20higher,each%20university's%20board%20of%20trustees.

VIEWPOINT 1

"Because of the overwhelming jumble of information and misinformation that surrounds us, a citizen without the kind of rangy mind the liberal arts cultivate is likely to have her citizenship hijacked."

Do the Humanities Make Students Better Employees and Citizens?

Kevin Reilly, Charles Steger, James Barker, and J. Bernard Machen

In this viewpoint, four former university presidents address the question of what role the humanities play in preparing students not only for the workforce, but to be engaged citizens who can tackle the social challenges of today. They discuss the types of skills that are acquired through humanities education and the ways they can complement a STEM education. Kevin Reilly is President Emeritus and Regent Professor of the University of Wisconsin, Madison. Charles Steger is President Emeritus of Virginia Tech. James Barker is President Emeritus and a professor of architecture at Clemson University. J. Bernard Machen is President Emeritus of the University of Florida.

"Why Do We Need the Humanities?," by Kevin Reilly, Charles Steger, James Barker, and J. Bernard Machen, The Conversation, March 16, 2015, https://theconversation.com/why-do-we-need-the-humanities-38640. Licensed under CC BY-ND 4.0 International.

The Future of Higher Education

As you read, consider the following questions:

1. According to Machen and Barker, what change has occurred to the core curriculum of universities over the past few decades?
2. According to Steger, how does designing public housing demonstrate the usefulness of a humanities education in careers that are not overtly related to the humanities?
3. According to Reilly, what skills that are developed through the humanities are employers looking for?

Search the word "humanities" online and up pops the phrase "humanities under attack." The majority of undergraduates today are majoring in business, science and technology disciplines. Technology—and its promise of being able to fix all problems—is, it seems, king.

What does all this mean for higher education? Why have the humanities undergone a crisis of legitimacy? And why does this matter?

We asked four former university presidents—of Clemson University, University of Florida, University of Wisconsin and Virginia Tech—to give us their perspectives on these questions.

Bernie Machen, University of Florida

Critical thinking, appreciation of the arts and humanities and understanding how to relate to society and the natural world are essential characteristics of the educated person.

Historically, the liberal arts and humanities have contributed to developing such a person. But there is real concern over how this is occurring in today's universities.

The decline in the number of students taking liberal arts majors (seven percent in 2013, according to the American Academy of Arts and Sciences) has at least three causes.

First, academia—especially public institutions of higher education—has deferred responsibility for directing the college curriculum. In the last 30 years, professional disciplines like business and engineering have eliminated core curricula and tailored courses to specific competencies.

Second, administrators and even state legislators have emphasized that general education (the traditional humanities "cores" like English and history) can be accounted for with credits from high school and community colleges. The focus of higher education then becomes preparation for a job.

And, third, the humanities and social sciences have not done enough to stimulate interest in their disciplines.

It took legislation at the state level to allow us at the University of Florida (UF) to get the humanities back into the curriculum through requiring of all students 12 hour credits of UF only "core courses."

Today every UF freshman has to take "What Is the Good Life?," a course that introduces its syllabus to students with the following paragraph:

> The question is especially relevant for a detailed examination as you become more and more involved in making the decisions that will shape your future and the future of others. In order to make reasonable, ethical, well-informed life choices, it is useful to reflect upon how one might aspire to live both as an individual, and a member of local and global communities.

Whatever happened to the recognition that a university education has at least three purposes: helping one understand who they are and what excites and motivates them; helping understand one's relationship to the greater world; and, also, becoming prepared for a job?

Jim Barker, Clemson University

Bernie Machen's analysis is spot on. The core curriculum has shrunk at public universities and general education is increasingly provided by community colleges. To counter this, Clemson (like the University of Florida and others) has developed new programs, in our case multi-disciplinary undergraduate research teams through the Creative Inquiry initiative.

Consider this. Apple Inc has now reached a market valuation of $770 billion: it is the world's most valuable company, worth more than Exxon and Berkshire Hathaway combined.

But as founder Steve Jobs himself said when launching the iPad in 2010: "It is in Apple's DNA that technology alone is not enough. It's technology married with liberal arts, married with the humanities, that yields the results that make our hearts sing."

In my experience, business leaders and employers recognize the value of this marriage and look for it in our graduates. It is clear that to thrive in a society where they may have up to six different careers, business and STEM graduates need also to be curious and creative, to be critical thinkers and good communicators.

My exemplar here is Clemson architecture graduate Carl Sobocinski whose renovation of historic buildings into restaurants has led to a remarkable urban revitalization of Greenville, South Carolina and to a career, for him, as a "serial entrepreneur" in the hospitality industry.

Charles Steger, Virginia Polytechnic Institute

The world is beset with complex and often intractable problems where unfortunately sub-optimization is often the best possible outcome.

Problem solving and the effective application of these solutions require that multiple dimensions of the human intellect be employed. These range from deductive reasoning to the exercise of substantive aesthetic judgment.

Consider, for example, the design of a public housing project.

For the design of the building itself, the square footage per family, structural design and fire code requirements are all known and quantifiable. Logical deductive reasoning is the perfect tool.

However, there are psychological, sociological, economic, and environmental dimensions with hundreds of variables. Many of these cannot be quantified and yet they need to be integrated into the solution if the project is to be successful. This is where the aesthetic judgment and informed intuition must complement deductive reasoning. The former, in turn, draw upon the ability to recognize complex patterns of association and key structuring variables which often change from problem to problem.

How are these additional capacities for reasoning developed? Through experience. Experiential learning exercises and experience, not lectures, strengthen the capacity to recognize complex patterns with many variables of high uncertainty. They inform the intuition.

The failure to incorporate studies in the liberal arts and humanities, along with STEM education, will deprive the next generation of students the critical thinking skills and context necessary to address the challenges they will face in the future.

Kevin Reilly, University of Wisconsin

George Bernard Shaw opined that all professions are a conspiracy against the laity.

Humanities faculty have too often conspired well. Insider jargon—like hermeneutics—is rife. Talking about "the epistemology of post-structuralist overdetermination" does not do much to excite most undergraduates about literature.

Ironically, this "insider trading" has occurred at the same time that the Western canon is being stretched to connect to contemporary popular culture in such domains as film, television, music, and the new social media. The next course title could be "James Joyce and Irish Cinematic Zombiism."

The apparent lack—in so many cases—of connective tissue joining the three elements of the curriculum—the major, general education, and electives—has further stoked anxiety that there is no common understanding of what an educated, 21st century American should know and be able to do.

But we do know. Employers send a consistent message about what they look for in a college-educated employee: the ability to write clearly, speak persuasively, analyze data effectively, work in diverse groups, and understand the competitive global knowledge environment.

These characteristics are all nurtured and tested in a purposeful liberal arts education. Employers want these capacities in their hires. And, critically, American democracy needs them in its citizens. Because of the overwhelming jumble of information and misinformation that surrounds us, a citizen without the kind of rangy mind the liberal arts cultivate is likely to have her citizenship hijacked.

There is, without doubt, a critical need to rethink and restructure the liberal arts core to help develop intellectually lively and engaged citizens and leaders. The good news is that this also constitutes an opportunity that society is looking to colleges and universities to seize.

VIEWPOINT 2

> "I don't have a problem with anti-racism or teaching about the history of race. What I don't support is critical race theory stuff." Anonymous survey respondent.

How the Debate on Diversity and Equity Came to Dominate Education

Matt Grossman, Carson Byrd, and Jonathan Collins

In this viewpoint, which is a transcript of the podcast The Science of Politics, *Matt Grossman explores the issue of diversity and equity in education politics. Grossman talks to Carson Bird about his research which found that while universities discuss diversity, equity, and inclusion, they often fall short of achieving racial equality due to underfunding, understaffing, and insufficient commitment. Jonathan Collins shares findings from his research which suggest that opposition to critical race theory (CRT) is driven by the term itself rather than the actual content. His research found that CRT has been weaponized in political debates. Matt Grossmann is Director of the Institute for Public Policy and Social Research (IPPSR) and a professor of political science at Michigan State University. Carson Byrd is faculty director of research initiatives for the National Center for Institutional Diversity at the University of Michigan and associate professor of sociology*

"How the debate over diversity and equity came to dominate education politics," by Matt Grossman, Carson Byrd, and Matthew Collins, Niskanen Center, March 22, 2023. https://www.niskanencenter.org/how-the-debate-over-diversity-and-equity-came-to-dominate-education-politics/. Licensed under CC-BY 4.0 International.

at the University of Louisville. Jonathan Collins is a professor of political science, public policy, and education at Brown University.

As you read, consider the following questions:

1. What are some of the challenges that Byrd identifies in the efforts of universities to achieve diversity, equity, and inclusion?
2. What is the key factor driving opposition to the teaching of critical race theory, according to Collins' research?
3. What are the key findings of Collins' public opinion research regarding antiracist teaching and critical race theory?

Republican governors like Ron DeSantis have elevated critiques about racial and gender politics in schools and universities to the center of American politics, quickly transforming both K–12 and higher education policy debates. What are schools and universities actually doing and why have critiques of critical race theory and educators gained such political power now? Carson Byrd finds that universities are not achieving racial equality, but they've still become the place for conservatives to react against cultural change. Jonathan Collins finds that critical race theory has become an effective bogeyman despite wide public support for teaching about racism in public schools. Both reflect on how these debates quickly became the center of our culture wars and merged K–12 and university politics.

Matt Grossmann: How Diversity and Equity Came to Dominate Education Politics, this week on the *Science of Politics*. For the Niskanen Center, I'm Matt Grossmann.

Republican governors like Ron DeSantis have elevated critiques about racial and gender politics in schools and universities to the center of American politics, quickly transforming both K–12 and higher education policy debates. What are schools and universities actually doing around diversity, equity, and inclusion and their curriculums, and why have critiques of critical race theory and educators gained such political power now?

This week, I talked to Carson Byrd of the University of Michigan about his book, *Behind the Diversity Numbers*. He finds that universities are not achieving racial equality, but have still become the place for conservatives to react against cultural change.

I also talked to Jonathan Collins of Brown University about his new paper, *They Only Hate the Term*. He finds that critical race theory has become an effective bogeyman despite wide public support for teaching about racism in public schools. Both reflect on how these debates quickly became the center of our culture wars and merged K–12 and university politics. Let's start with the higher education controversy where Carson Byrd has been studying what universities are actually up to.

So your latest book critiques university strategies in the diversity, equity and inclusion area. So tell us what universities are actually doing here and why it's not living up to the bill.

Carson Byrd: Sure. We see a lot of discussions about diversity, equity, and inclusion in higher ed. And obviously, politically, we see a lot of critiques of it. But one of the biggest impediments is kind of underestimating how much needs to be done on a college campus to overcome different obstacles to student success, for example. So some of this is resulting in underfunding and understaffing, which is a big issue. So not actually committing the necessary resources and personnel to achieving some of these big games. And others are not thinking big enough, right, where they might just have a series of celebratory events about different kinds of moments in time or for different communities. And while these are really important, they don't do the full job. Right?

So while many universities have kind of improved what they do to increase access and success among students when they arrive, they're not always consistent. And there's always a constant need for additional programming and support services and adjustments that haven't been done before.

So a lot of the critique that my book and my work, in general, put out there is that we need to be attentive to the details and be open to more changes, but just more serious reflections about where we are and where we need to go. And that's not to say that universities aren't doing a lot of things, but it's just a ... It's been inconsistent, if you will.

Matt Grossmann: So how are universities measuring their diversity, equity, and inclusion efforts? Is this just a case of counting who's in what roles, and then maybe surveys for kind of attitudinal-type measures, and is there any better way to evaluate the success?

Carson Byrd: So the short and sweet answer is there's a multitude of ways that people can measure components to diversity, equity, and inclusion. And again, they're not always consistent. Some of the most common ones that we think of is student and faculty representation. How many students are identified as Black or Latino on campus? What percentage of students are identified with those groups, right? Those are some of the most common measurements.

The changes also reflect a difference in understanding what accountability, in the legal context, of different institutions are. In the state of Michigan, it's an Affirmative Action banned state. So what exactly is measured and why has a different context than in the Commonwealth of Virginia that is not an Affirmative Action banned state. Right? So these measurements have a very sociopolitical context that allows institutions to do certain things or not, or have responsibilities and accountability to do that.

Some of these measurements are retention rates ... to understand how successful a campus is at supporting students from different backgrounds. Graduation rates four and six years ... Sometimes we say, "Hey, it'd be great if all of our students graduated in four years, but we know that that doesn't always happen." And sometimes it's not just about students having to

Can Higher Education Help Address Social Issues?

work more because they come from low income backgrounds or they have other family responsibilities. Sometimes we haven't actually recognized that our programs aren't set up for students to effectively graduate in four years, that they might have to take a fifth year or maybe a sixth year if there's certain kinds of internship

Learning to Be Good Citizens

Research conducted by the Student Research Group turned up something troubling about what students are learning in most American high schools. An important outlook, "Global Citizenship," is not being sufficiently addressed or developed.

American high school students are learning to be top academic performers. Many are learning the knowledge they need to major in STEM and other careers in college. Yet at a time when the ability to work with people from other cultures will become increasingly important, most high schools seem to have focused their priorities elsewhere.

To quote from our State of the Union 2018 report . . .

"The economy is inherently global – connected by instantaneous data and rapidly accelerating, disruptive change – yet only half of students believe high school is preparing them to be responsible global citizens. Students more often say high school is preparing them for local citizenship."

What Kinds of Citizens Are Our Schools Developing?

Yet that doesn't mean that high schools are failing to prepare students for other kinds of good citizenship. The research finds that schools are preparing . . .

- 68% of students to be good local citizens
- 66% of students to be good digital citizens
- 51% or students to be good global citizens
- 39% of students to be good national citizens

"Research Finds that Only 51% or U.S. High School Students Are Learning to Be Good Global Citizens," Student Research Group, June 14, 2018.

requirements. Or if you look at some of the programs that are in the College of Engineering here and at other institutions, those are actually a little bit more lengthy programs than perhaps some of these measures are out there. So it's kind of hard sometimes to see exactly what is going on.

And as you alluded to, there's also survey measures about student experiences and everyday life with campus climates and engagement. Much less so, we collect data that is more qualitative and open-ended to find out about people's experiences. And so there's a lot of data that's out there, but sometimes, and oftentimes, it's inconsistent or [inaudible 00:11:18] connected to or less connected to each other so that we can tell a more holistic story of what's going on our campuses. So that makes it really hard to be able to speak to how effective certain kinds of policies or programs might be because we're not necessarily monitoring with data as much as we would like to be.

Matt Grossmann: So I guess I'll play a little bit more devil's advocate on this. So there does seem to be a potential meeting of the minds in some of the left and right critiques of this effort, which is on the left we say, "Well, you're doing the easy stuff," and maybe doing something where you can have everybody go to a training, you put something on your website, establish a new office. But look at your progress or lack thereof in actually diversifying your faculty or top leadership positions.

And then on the right, sometimes expressed in similar terms is that this is not actually about achieving a particular end of diversity. This is about getting everybody to parrot the same rhetoric, rather than actually achieve that end. So is there any danger to pursuing a lot of diversity, equity and inclusion efforts in name and getting pretty poor results?

Carson Byrd: Absolutely. If you're not committed fully to these things, you're almost always going to fail. And I think that's something that's really important for university administrators and the public at large to consider. If you don't go 100% at these things, how much progress you're going to make is probably going to be pretty minimal. And in some cases, depending on how things are set up, you could actually do more damage because you haven't thought through all these different issues. This is part of what is also really hard about measuring progress is we think about equity, we think about inclusion as goals, as benchmarks and not as processes that we're always going to have to work on these things because things always change. And that's really challenging for people who are just like, "Have we done it yet, or not? Have we succeeded or not?" And as much as I would like to say, "Yeah, I'm with you, or we've succeeded on these things," it doesn't actually mean that something else hasn't changed that we need to be attentive to in these same conversations. Obstruction is a big thing. If we know that we need certain kinds of resources to support students or faculty, and you don't get those, then obviously you're going to be curtailing the results that you're wanting.

There's also a very dangerous kind of game that's played that because we know in general that the deck, if you will, is kind of stacked up against diversity, equity, and inclusion efforts in higher education and organizations as a whole, that it could reinforce racially, essentialist, and biologically determinist beliefs about different communities. We already see how people have talked about affirmative action as, "We want qualified applicants." As if people taking into consideration the fullest extent of the human experience, and that people are still attacked and excluded from different opportunities and yet are still succeeding, that those experiences aren't important to take into account by saying, "Well, we want qualified applicants." You're also saying that you really don't care about people. That you're not really wanting to think about these things, that you view people as incapable or unworthy. And this has come up again and again around affirmative action in DEI.

So the latest wave that we're seeing is just yet another one that we've always had about opening up higher education and opportunity for those who have always been, or have mostly been excluded in different eras. So yeah, there can be a lot of issues for not fulfilling certain kinds of benchmarks or desired outcomes, but we also have to say, what did people have to begin with? And also when we measure progress, we could say, 'Well, look how diverse our campus is in the year 2023." Back in 1922, 100 years ago it wasn't like that. And it was like, do you understand the context of what 1922 or '23 actually was? Do you understand how much of a bad comparison 100 years, beginning to end, really is? Politically, resource wise? There's so many things that are different, but we make these really bad comparisons to try to set things up as saying, "Well, we've made a lot of progress," when really it's a relative kind of comparison that's being made to discount how much more work is needed to achieve some of these goals that we're setting out for higher education.

Matt Grossmann: Are conservative politicians just representing real public opinion? And what can we learn about the debate over racial issues in K–12 education? Jonathan Collins argues that the public supports most teaching about race, but opposition has been successfully mobilized around fear of critical race theory.

So your new paper enters this heated discussion over teaching critical race theory, arguing that they only hate the term. That this is really about just that term rather than the teaching of the content. So what's the evidence for that, and is this really just about what we call it?

Jonathan Collins: Well, that's a great question. So the paper is maybe perhaps a bit of an oversell of what's happening here. Well, the title in and of itself is probably a little bit of an oversell. But what was happening was I started doing these national surveys, trying to get a sense of how people were feeling about some of the most hot buttoned education policy issues. And this was starting back in 2020, and I wanted to know … I'm a net policy scholar. I want to know how the public feels about some of the leading education policy issues. And at the time, anti-racist teaching was starting to enter the public sphere, the national conversation. Ibram X. Kendi had released his book, *How to Be an Anti-Racist*, the George Floyd protests had happened, and the conversation on anti-racism and anti-Black racism had become one of the leading national issues. And so I was curious about how people were digesting some of the leading education policy issues with this as the backdrop.

And so literally one of the last questions I ended up throwing onto the survey was this question about whether or not people support anti-racist teaching. Because again, this is 2020. It seemed like, "Okay, there's some conversation happening around this. People seem to be starting to form preferences around this. At least that's what I'm seeing from the media and social media."

And so I asked this question about anti-racist teaching, and if people support the idea of teaching about the history of race in America and the schools, and I get the results back and it's pretty strong support, over 80% support from the respondents. And I'm like, it seems like this is much more of a polarized debate, again, nationally and the media and the social media. But then I'm looking at these survey results and they seem to suggest that there's relative uniform support.

And so I do replication. I filled it again in 2021, a few months later, and I get virtually the same results. And again, one of the things that I also did was I embedded an experimental component to this. So I thought, well, if there's something that is influencing support or opposition here, it might be parental consent. So I thought people would be opposed, especially white parents would be opposed to the idea of anti-racist teaching in the schools taught without parental consent. And so half of the participants were randomly assigned this additional language that anti-racist teaching would be happening without parental consent. Even with this additional language, no results. I still saw really strong support for anti-racist teaching.

And then I got a direct message. So one of the survey respondents while taking the 2021 version, sends me this a message and says, "Hey, I don't have a problem with anti-racism or teaching about the history of race. What I don't support is this critical race theory stuff." And then a light bulb went up. And so I had ran another replication, and the treatment this time was literally the same question with just the term critical race theory added into the text. And then suddenly I started to see pretty major differences in supporter opposition for anti-racist teaching. And so that becomes the sort of title of the paper, which is they only hate the term because when the term critical race theory is literally just added into this sentence about supporting anti-racist teaching, then the support for anti-racist teaching declines significantly.

Matt Grossmann: So one reading of that is that it's about the term itself. One other potential divider though is what are we teaching history and it's a contemporary influence? Are we teaching something that's about kind of current policy and politics? And so critical race theory might kind of bring that to mind for people in a way that teaching about slavery and discrimination as history does not. So what do you think about that divide? Is this about history versus current politics and policy, or about this particular theory?

Jonathan Collins: So I think it's an open question and it's debatable, right? So what do I think is happening? I think that there's been this politicization around the term and that politicization is filtering into what I'm finding in my results. And the thing that gives me even more confidence in believing this is when you look at some of the other public opinion polling that has been done around critical race theory, especially over the last year. Plus the consistent thing that people seem to be finding is that there are still a lot of people who don't know what critical race theory is. I think it was UMass put out a poll and they found it close to 40% of their respondents who they asked about critical race theory said that they didn't know. They weren't familiar with it.

Ed Week has an article where they looked at exit polls from some of the elections that were happening in 2021, and they were finding similar things. There was a sizable, if not majority, of the survey respondents were saying that they were somewhat unfamiliar with the term critical race theory. And so I think for it to have this interpretation of being about current politics, there would have to be more knowledge and therefore salience around it. And we just are not really seeing strong evidence of that. And what we are seeing though are these very strong partisan differences. And so even in the Amherst poll, I think it was slightly more than 50% of Republicans opposed critical race theory, the teaching of critical race theory in schools. And it was like less than 25%, I believe for Democrats. In my study, I find a similar gap about 30 percentage point difference between Republicans and the average from just framing this idea of critical race theory or just introducing the term into the conversation. And so I think it's possible amongst that this is a minority of folks on the right who are thinking about this, thinking about critical race theory as a current phenomenon. But I think what we're seeing from a modal standpoint are just people who don't really have clear knowledge of what it is, solidified preferences around it, and therefore I think they're tapping into a partisanship and ideology.

VIEWPOINT 3

> *"It has become even more important to reflect on the role of HE [higher education] in forging civic-mindedness among its students, as well as the type of education and skills that should be more relevant for the development of HE."*

Valuing the Civic Role of University Education
Pedro Nuno Teixeira and Manja Klemenčič

In this viewpoint, the authors posit that higher education's contribution to the development of students is much broader than job and career preparation. Higher education correlates to improved health, improved education prospects for children, and greater longevity. They also note the effect of higher education in strengthening citizenship and participation in democratic institutions. Although the relationship between education and civic behavior is not straightforward, there is strong empirical evidence that education correlates with community participation and a greater likelihood to join organizations. The political behavior of individuals is also influenced by education, with educated people more likely to vote, follow political campaigns, and volunteer for community issues. Pedro Nuno Teixeira is Director of the Center for Research in Higher Education Policies and associate professor of economics at the University of Porto in Portugal. Manja

---

"Valuing the Civic Role of University Education in an Age of Competition and Rapid Change," by Pedro Nuno Teixeira and Manja Klemenčič, *Springer Nature*, September 2, 2021. https://link.springer.com/chapter/10.1007/978-3-030-67245-4_23. Licensed under CC-BY 4.0 International.

Can Higher Education Help Address Social Issues?

Klemenčič is an associate senior lecturer in the department of sociology at Harvard University.

As you read, consider the following questions.
1. What are some of the quantitative and qualitative impacts of higher education?
2. According to this viewpoint, should universities be sites of citizenship?
3. What arguments do the authors make for students to get involved in civic activities?

In recent decades the discourse about higher education (HE) has been dominated by an instrumentalist view that emphasized the labour market benefits for graduates and the net (social) returns to tax payers for the public funding of HE (Psacharopoulos and Patrinos 2010). Nonetheless, HE's contribution to students' development and life is much broader than that through several non-market benefits to graduates, including improved health, improved education prospects for children, and greater longevity (see McMahon 2009). Furthermore, the effects of HE are visible in many civic dimensions, such as strengthened citizenship and civic mindedness and participation in democratic institutions. Thus, in this chapter, we discuss the significance of the civic contribution of HE beyond a narrow version of economic effects and on education practices that foster students' civic mindedness and civic engagement.

Beyond a Narrow Understanding of the Economic Benefits of Higher Education

The development of human capital theory in the mid-twentieth century anchored education as a central tenet of individual and social wealth and contributed to a massive increase in HE worldwide. Though the average private return to HE continued to be very attractive, there is significant evidence of a growing differentiation among groups of graduates and of the unequal benefits to each of them (Oreopoulos and Petronijevic 2013). The acceleration of technological change is also having an impact on the relevance of existing stocks and profiles of human capital (Aoun 2017), which will also affect qualified workers and selective occupations (and not only low-skilled workers). This has stimulated increasing debate about the skills and competencies that HE should develop in students. If we add to these trends the impact of the great recession and the challenging political and social context that has been emerging in many countries over recent years, the need to rethink the benefits of HE more broadly through the so-called nonmonetary benefits becomes more apparent (McMahon 2009).

Both the developments in the labour market and the aforementioned challenges of social cohesion and political fragmentation emphasise the importance of the role of HE shaping civic beliefs and attitudes. The relationship between education and civic behaviour is not straightforward. Education increases income and therefore raises the opportunity cost of civic activities vis-à-vis productive ones. Thus, greater investments in education increase the returns in the labour market and create a lower incentive for civic activity. However, there is also an educational impact on developing cultural attitudes and the link between the educational system and values. Each of these forces will differ according to the institution attended, the field of study or type of degree, since each of these dimensions will entail different educational experiences and different opportunities for graduates in the labour market.

Generally speaking, education's impact on citizenship has quantitative and qualitative aspects. On the one hand, education encourages broader participation by increasing interest and knowledge of civic issues. On the other hand, education enhances the quality of civic participation by equipping people with cognitive skills that enable their capacity to play a more critical and effective role. There is strong empirical evidence between education and a variety of social outcomes associated with civic values, including a greater likelihood to join organizations and participate in community activities (Glaeser et al. 2007). Although the effects may correlate with other factors, such as family and social background, they are sufficiently strong even when controlling for that.

One of the areas being studied in social and civic benefits of education refers to political participation and engagement. The impact of education on voting behaviour is one of the best documented aspects in political behaviour, with various recent studies showing that more educated individuals are more likely to vote (Dee 2004; Milligan et al. 2004). Education reduces the costs of certain forms of civic engagement and increases the perceived benefits of civic engagement. More educated individuals are more likely to register to vote, to follow political campaigns and political affairs, to attend political meetings, to volunteer for community issues or to attend community meetings. Moreover, they also tend to have a more favourable judgement about politics, its relevance, and the value of involvement in the political process, that may contribute to a better polity. HE contributes to promoting engaged and alert citizenship. This is referred to as critical citizens (Norris 2010), i.e., individuals who support and value democratic ideals but present at the same time significant levels of dissatisfaction with the performance of the political system.

Civic virtues may transcend political participation and refer to greater trust in institutions or others or the willingness to accept and tolerate diversity (Borgonovi 2012). Trust and tolerance are attitudes or ways of being that have consequences on social cohesion (Glaeser et al. 2007). More open, diverse, and tolerant societies have a greater capacity for innovation and entrepreneurship as tolerance can manifest itself in the creation of bonds of trust, either interpersonal or in the institutions themselves.

Although the accumulation of evidence about a strong and positive relationship between HE and civic behaviour is important, it is even more relevant to understand the mechanisms by which that link operates. That is getting inside the so-called black-box of HE. There is some exploratory evidence that certain types of skills and disciplines seem to strongly correlate with political participation more than others (Hillygus 2005). However, we do not know how comparable those individuals were regarding their characteristics and preferences and to what extent individuals that chose certain fields are different in their social and political attitudes and values. Moreover, it is relevant to discuss how much those individuals had comparable experiences in HE (the type of education, content, learning methods) and the extent to which differences in those experiences could be relevant in shaping their political values and engagement.

Revaluing the Civic Role of University Education

We can explore the civic role of HE through two main approaches. The capabilities approach (Sen 1999) submits that freedom to achieve wellbeing, which is of primary moral importance, is to be understood in terms of people's capabilities which are real opportunities to do and to be what they reason to value. Nussbaum (2010) suggests that the capabilities that are crucial for the internal health of democracies are critical thinking, global citizenship dispositions, and empathetic understanding of human experiences, and it is education's task to equip students with these capabilities. We can also consider the civic effects of HE through the lens of normative democratic theory, especially regarding what is reasonable to expect from universities in guiding the design or development of democratic institutions. As well as the democratic practices within different social institutions, including universities (Biesta 2010). At the same time, educating future legislators, since a college degree is one advantage of getting elected to a legislative body (Hillygus 2005). The question here is how universities can help develop or foster democratic practices in their societies or help combat illiberal democratic practices. Both the capabilities approach and normative democratic theory are closely related in the context of education of students for civic mindedness and participation in democratic institutions. While the civic role of universities should, in principle, encompass all areas of operations, we are particularly interested in how that role can be better fulfilled through the function of education. That is, by strengthening student civic engagement and civic-mindedness.

Elite HE with small class cohorts undoubtedly provides better conditions for impairing civic values while nurturing students' individuality and autonomy in civic expression. In mass HE, the tendency is towards the standardization of education provision which lends itself better to indoctrination rather than individuality in civic mindedness (McFarlane 2017). Yet, standardized practices towards educating civically minded students, such as variations of mandatory civic courses, seem to be counterproductive to those objectives. Nonetheless, there are several examples of good practices in several networks and university initiatives that constitute the "global engaged higher education" movement (Watson et al. 2011). Major examples include the Talloires Network, an international association of over 400 universities committed to strengthening the civic roles and social responsibilities of higher education (Watson et al. 2011); and the Campus Compact, an organization based in the U.S. dedicated to promoting civic purposes of higher education (Battistoni 2017). The most vocal proponent of education for democracy and diversity in Europe has been the Council of Europe. Other national or regional networks have emerged over the past two decades in the United Kingdom, Ireland, Australia, South Africa, and the Arab world.

The enactment of civic mission through education is by no means uncontested. It is intertwined with the persistent debate about what should be taught and to what purpose. Looking at the aim of education serving democracy by strengthening civic mindedness in students, there are notable differences between the classical and progressive traditions (for an excellent review see Sant 2019). The classical tradition, i.e., the tradition of liberal learning, is in favour of education serving democracy but in a way that is disengaged from current life (Oakenshott 1989). Students are asked to delve deep into classical works of world civilizations and explore the ways of knowing, critically examine, and deliberate about democratic traditions and its core themes. Including conceptions of liberty, theories of democracy, and principles of distributive justice. In contrast, progressive educational tradition argues in favour of appraising the knowledge of the past for its relevance to solving the social problems of present times. The progressive educationalists advocate for the revision of curricula in line with critical, deliberative, and action-centred pedagogies. In a milder variation of progressive education, teachers are asked to help students develop civic mindedness and civic agency in any course, regardless of discipline, by introducing meaningful topics and activities that make connections to the real world (Boyte 2008).

The globally engaged university movement follows both educational traditions. The trend has not been to offer specific civic education courses in HE, but instead to offer courses that purposefully include civic competence-building to balance the disciplinary courses (Zgaga 2016). Moreover, students are involved in political and civic deliberations, contestations, and actions on campus (Biesta 2010). Students are also guided into co-curricular and extracurricular activities, such as community volunteering, paid internships, student leadership, and other types of volunteer or paid activities in the domain of public service or community engagement (Cress et al. 2013). These public service activities can be directed to communities outside the campus, as well as directly serve university communities. Student service to their university community is considered highly impactful for overall positive student experience and wellbeing (Kuh 2008). Furthermore, by providing opportunities for civic engagement on campus, universities can significantly enhance students' civic agency (Boyte 2008). Regardless of the students' motivations to engage in public service roles—be that altruistic or CV-building— students inevitably gain some civic mindedness through exposure to issues and other civic minded individuals.

Finally, the informal (or incidental) learning for civic mindedness is associated with the notion of universities as "sites of citizenship" (Bergan 2004). Universities transmit values and attitudes through the ways of doing and through issues to which they give more or less attention (Klemenčič 2010). One such value is enabling student governments as a distinct form of political institutions within universities that organize, aggregate, and represent student interests (Klemenčič 2020). Another, more contested, is acceptance of (non-violent) student activism as a form of political expression. Yet, the education practices at universities have shifted from democratic principles of governance into more corporate models that undermine the civic roles of students through representation, and pay more attention to individual student rights. Such changes undermine the notions of universities as sites of citizenship and civic engagement and deprive students of civic opportunities that would strengthen their civic mindedness, and dispositions for (university) citizenship and civic engagement.

Concluding Remarks

Higher education is facing important challenges regarding its societal role. For many decades, the sector's relentless expansion was largely supported by the belief in the income and employment benefits of a degree. Universities were assessed regarding their contribution to that goal. Nonetheless, rapid and substantial changes in the labour market, and important crises and tensions in many countries (amplified by the current pandemic), have underlined the need to consider the contribution of HE to individuals and society more broadly. Particularly in times of increasing social change and tensions, it has become even more important to reflect on the role of HE in forging civic-mindedness among its students, as well as the type of education and skills that should be more relevant for the development of HE.

Practices to foster civic mindedness in HE students are diverse and demonstrate a commitment to experiential learning that is not confined to classrooms but can take place anywhere on campus and in engagement with community partners. These practices also express the conception of students as partners in knowledge generation and as full members, indeed university citizens, contributing to university communities. As we have tried to argue, promoting civic mindedness should be regarded less as an additional element in education that can be promoted in a standard way, but rather as something that pervades the missions and governance of the institution, which, therefore, needs to be integrated and adapted to the individual profile and circumstances of the institution. This is especially relevant given the growing stratification/differentiation in many HE systems. Meaning that the type of education that students receive can be very different.

With the growing erosion of trust and social bonds (Pharr and Putnam 2000), and with growing political polarization, there are very few social institutions left with the capacity and vitality of HE to nurture civic values and promote critical citizenry. This needs to be addressed in the framework of HE's specificity and mission and the diversity of students they serve, namely the type of degree, the field, or other major characteristics of the student body. Universities should also strive to understand their impact effects through students' civic engagement and the extent to which innovative approaches can strengthen the nexus between HE and civic virtues. This will require universities to articulate a long-term strategy that places multidimensional social development at the core of its mission.

References

Aoun, Joseph (2017). Robot-Proof: Higher Education in the Age of Artificial Intelligence. MIT Press.

Battistoni, R. M. (2017). *Civic Engagement Across the Curriculum: A Resource Book for Service - Learning Faculty in All Disciplines*. Boston, Massachusetts: Campus Compact.

Bergan, S. (2004). *The University as Res Publica: Higher education governance, student participation and the university as a site of citizenship*. Strasbourg: Council of Europe Publishing.

Borgonovi, F. (2012). The relationship between education and levels of trust and tolerance in Europe. *The British Journal of Sociology*, 63(1), 146-167.

Biesta, G.J.J. (2010). How to Exist Politically and Learn from It: Hannah Arendt and the Problem of Democratic Education. *Teachers College Record, 112* (2), 558–577.

Boyte, H. C. (2008). Against the current: Developing the civic agency of students. *Change: The Magazine of Higher Learning, 40*(3), 8-15.

Cress, C.M., Collier,P.J., Reitenauer, V.L., & Associates. (2013). *Learning through serving: A student guidebook for service-learning and civic engagement across academic disciplines and cultural communities.* (2nd ed.), Expanded. Sterling: Stylus.

Dee, T.S. (2004). Are There Civic Returns to Education? *Journal of Public Economics, 88*, 1697–1720.

Glaeser, E.L., Ponzetto, G.A.M., & Shleifer, A. (2007). Why does democracy need education?. *J Econ Growth, 12*,77–99.

Hillygus, D. (2005). The Missing Link: Exploring the Relationship Between Higher Education and Political Engagement. *Political Behavior, 27*(1), 25-47.

Klemenčič, M. (2010). Higher education for democratic citizenship. In E.Fromet, (Ed.), *EUA Bologna Handbook: Making Bologna work,* B 1.3-1. Berlin: Raabe.

Klemenčič M. (2020). Student Governments. In Teixeira P., Shin J. (Eds). *Encyclopedia of International Higher Education Systems and Institutions.* Springer, Dordrecht.

Kuh, G.D. (2008). High-impact educational practices: What they are, who has access to them, and why they matter. Washington, DC: Association of American Colleges & Universities.

McFarlane, B. (2017) *Freedom to learn: The threat to student academic freedom and why it needs to be reclaimed.* London: Routledge.

McMahon, W. (2009). *Higher Learning Greater Good: The Private and Social Benefits of Higher Education.* Baltimore: Johns Hopkins University Press.

Milligan, K., Moretti, E., & Oreopoulos. P. (2004). Does education improve citizenship? Evidence from the United States and the United Kingdom. *Journal of Public Economics, 88*(9-10), 1667-1695.

Norris, P. (2010). *Democratic Deficit: Critical Citizens Revisited.* Cambridge University Press, Cambridge.

Nussbaum, M. C. (2010). *Not for Profit: Why Democracy Needs the Humanities.* Princeton, N.J: Princeton University Press.

Oakenshott, M. (1989). *The Voice of Liberal Learning.* New Haven: Yale University Press.

Oreopoulos, P. & Petronijevic, U. (2013). Making college worth it: A review of the returns to higher education. *The Future of Children*, 23(1):41–65.

Pharr, S., & Putnam, R. D. (2000). *Disaffected Democracies.* Princeton University Press, Princeton, NJ.

Psacharopoulos, G., & Patrinos, H. A. (2010). Human Capital and Rates of Returns, In Johnes&Johnes (Eds.) *International Handbook on the Economics of Education,* pp. 1-57.

Sant, E. (2019). Democratic Education: A Theoretical Review (2006-2017). *Review of Educational Research 89*(5), 655-696.

Sen, A. (1999).*Development as Freedom.* Oxford University Press.

Watson, D., Hollister. R., Stroud. S. E., & Babcock. E., (2011). *The engaged university: International perspectives on civic engagement.* London: Routledge.

Zgaga. P. (2016). Higher Education and Democratic Citizenship. In: Shin J., Teixeira. P. (Eds) *Encyclopedia of International Higher Education Systems and Institutions.* Springer, Dordrecht.

VIEWPOINT 4

> *"These more diverse environments have proved to reduce bias and promote peer acceptance."*

Why Diversity, Equity, and Inclusion Programs Benefit Colleges

Erica Jacqueline Licht

In this viewpoint, Erica Jacqueline Licht explains that although diversity, equity, and inclusion (DEI) programs have been accused of prioritizing racial identity over academic merit, this is far from true. In fact, she asserts, DEI programs actually have a beneficial impact on learning environments, with advantages including improved academic performance. Schools with DEI programs tend to have more satisfied students and faculty, more socially engaged classroom environments, and students who are more prepared for leadership after graduation. Erica Jacqueline Licht is the research project director of the Institutional Antiracism and Accountability Project at Harvard Kennedy School.

As you read, consider the following questions:

1. According to Licht, why are faculty more satisfied at schools with DEI programs?

"5 Ways that College Campuses Benefit from Diversity, Equity and Inclusion Programs," by Erica Jacqueline Licht, The Conversation, September 12, 2023, https://theconversation.com/5-ways-that-college-campuses-benefit-from-diversity-equity-and-inclusion-programs-208905. Licensed under CC BY-ND 4.0 International.

2. According to this viewpoint, how can DEI programs make the college curriculum more engaging?
3. In what ways are students who went to colleges and universities with DEI programs more engaged in their communities, according to Licht?

For more than half a century, colleges and universities have relied on dedicated programs to attract students of color and support them. Today, those programs—known as diversity, equity and inclusion, or DEI, programs—are under attack.

Republican lawmakers assail the programs as being driven by liberal Democrats' "woke agenda" to value and prioritize racial identity over merit. However, rigorous social science research shows that these programs result in universities with better student learning.

As a researcher who is concerned with racial equity on campus, I contend these are five ways DEI programs have made a difference at colleges and universities throughout the U.S.

Students Perform Better Academically

Students from marginalized identity groups—including Black, Indigenous, Latinx and Asian students, as well as first-generation students—perform better academically at schools with diversity programs, and graduate at a higher rate.

As a result of DEI programs, students also report feeling more included on campus through dedicated resources and spaces for students of color.

This sense of belonging also increases when, as a part of DEI programs, more faculty of color are hired.

When students feel like they belong, they stay in school and graduate after four years at a higher rate than those who do not.

Students Are Less Biased

Diversity programs have been shown to create more racially diverse learning environments.

These more diverse environments have proved to reduce bias and promote peer acceptance. Increased contact between students from different racial groups results in increased understanding of different perspectives and development of trust.

Students of color also report less racial stress and fewer feelings of imposter syndrome on campus.

More Satisfied Faculty

Faculty at schools with DEI programs including mentorship stay at their jobs longer and are more satisfied at their places of work. This increased job satisfaction is because of how DEI programs restructure university policies on hiring, promotion and advancement. This restructuring includes redesigning job descriptions, including more voices in the interview process and requiring implicit bias training for search committees.

Additionally, these changes result in increasing the number of junior faculty of color on campus.

More Engaging Curriculum and Classrooms

DEI programs produce more engaged scholarship, which results in higher quality of curriculum and classroom learning as reported by students themselves.

Faculty on campuses with greater curricular innovation publish higher quality work on issues that affect the communities in which their students will live and work.

Engaged academic work connects classroom learning to issues that students experience directly themselves, such as racism and discrimination based on class, gender and sexuality.

Students Are More Prepared to Be Local Leaders

As a result of DEI programs, students are more engaged in their communities after they graduate.

Additionally, students are more likely to participate in local government and politics, including turning out to vote and running for office after graduation.

Graduating students at schools with DEI programs are also more likely to have interracial friendships and are more prepared for multiracial professional settings because they gain a better understanding of race and ethnicity.

DEI programs have been time-tested as changing campuses for the better and attracting more Black, Indigenous, Latinx and Asian students. With race-based admissions having been outlawed, going forward DEI efforts can play an even greater role in attracting more students of color and creating the conditions for them to thrive.

Periodical and Internet Sources Bibliography

The following articles have been selected to supplement the diverse views presented in this chapter.

Ian Bogost, "America Will Sacrifice Anything for The College Experience," the *Atlantic*, October 20, 2020. https://www.theatlantic.com/technology/archive/2020/10/college-was-never-about-education/616777/.

Emma Bowman, "Here's What Happened When Affirmative Action Ended in California Public Colleges," NPR, June 3, 2023. https://www.npr.org/2023/06/30/1185226895/heres-what-happened-when-affirmative-action-ended-at-california-public-colleges.

Katherine Mangan, "Public Good or Public Threat? What Two Governors' Contrasting Platforms Say About Polarized Views of Colleges," the *Chronicle of Higher Education*, October 19, 2022. https://www.chronicle.com/article/public-good-or-public-threat.

Grace Mayer, "How Regional Public Colleges Benefit Their Communities," the *Chronicle of Higher Education*, October 20, 2022. https://www.chronicle.com/article/how-public-regional-universities-benefit-their-communities.

Angel B. Perez, "Employers Benefitted from Affirmative Action. It's Time To Step Up," *New York Times*, July 2, 2023. https://www.nytimes.com/2023/07/02/opinion/employers-colleges-affirmative-action.html?smid=nytcore-ios-share&referringSource=articleShare.

Henry Huiyao Wang, "Globalizations Isn't Dead, It's Just Not American Anymore," *Bloomberg*, March 6, 2022. https://www.bloomberg.com/opinion/articles/2022-05-07/u-s-china-cold-war-hasn-t-killed-globalization-yet?srnd=premium.

CHAPTER 4

What Rights Are Protected in Higher Education?

Chapter Preface

Free speech, student activism, and the creation/ownership of knowledge are traditionally associated with academia and now face new challenges in the U.S. These challenges are exacerbated by the popularity of social media, the decline in traditional media, particularly newspapers, and the intensification of debate about the role of universities and colleges in American society.

In considering the place of free speech and activism on college campuses, we should understand that historically, universities have been harbingers and promoters of societal change—from the student and faculty social and political protests of the 1960s to the #MeToo and Black Lives Matter protests of the 21st century. Such activism comes from the long-held belief that college campuses are places for the free expression of *all* ideas, and students should be allowed to express and be exposed to a variety of diverse viewpoints. The 21st century, however, has seen a strong rise in anti-free speech and relatedly anti-activist sentiments with the expressed belief that colleges should protect students from offensive and 'harmful' viewpoints. Of particular concern to proponents of this perspective is student activism around issues such as Black Lives Matter, LBGTQIA+ rights, abortion, and the #MeToo movement. Student protests around controversial speakers on campus like Milo Yiannopoulos [1] have ignited heated debates amongst Left and Right leaning constituents on college campuses in particular, and American society in general, highlighted by heated rhetoric among politicians and among the liberal and conservative media.

In this context, the political and ideological differences of the so-called "culture wars" in the 21st century United States are of note, as the political Left and political Right disagree about what should be taught and the overall role of higher education. Although the roots of the culture wars can be traced to the social and political movements of the 1960s, when student and academic voices were raised in support of civil rights and women's rights, ideological differences have intensified in the 21st century as the U.S. becomes more polarized and divisions deepen.[2]

While today there are deepening divisions over the place of free speech and activism on college and university campuses, another battle is being played out in a less public sphere but with equally far-reaching implications—the battle over the creation and ownership of knowledge. Universities have traditionally been spaces where knowledge is created, and innovation fostered, with discoveries shared freely in the public domain. Increasingly today, large corporations control research they co-fund at university campuses, and academic findings often are patented for commercial purposes. At a time when unprecedentedly large amounts of information are available on the internet, academic innovations become proprietary and removed from the public domain. Academic knowledge, which in general used to be freely shared, is now stifled, raising flags from faculty and librarians. One ray of hope comes from the growth of open access publishing, which offers a model where research findings are freely available to all. At the time of this writing, artificial intelligence also offers challenges and hope for the free availability of knowledge.

The viewpoints in this chapter present opposing perspectives on the above themes, guiding readers in a nuanced consideration of the issues, challenges and opportunities around free speech, student activism, and the creation and ownership of knowledge.

References

1. Sharmila Pixy Ferris and Kathleen Waldron. *Higher Education Leadership: Pathways and Insights*, 2021. Bingley, UK: Emerald Publishing.
2. Carlos Diaz Ruiz and Tomas Nilsson. "Disinformation And Echo Chambers: How Disinformation Circulates on Social Media Through Identity Driven Controversies," *Journal of Public Policy and Marketing*, 2022. https://journals.sagepub.com/doi/10.1177/07439156221103852.

VIEWPOINT 1

> *"When students do not have the luxury of just being students… They take on more than their fair share of commitment to improving the community."*

A Student Should Have the Privilege of Just Being a Student
ACUI

This viewpoint presents a summary of a research study conducted by six scholars from diverse backgrounds. Their research sheds light on the challenges student activists face when navigating institutional oppression and interacting with administrators and educators, including adverse impacts on their academic performance, isolation from peers and family, and physical and emotional exhaustion. The researchers found that student activists from minority backgrounds who work to combat institutional oppression personally grappled with racial battle fatigue, burnout, and compassion fatigue. Concerningly, these student activists also missed out on educational experiences. The researchers argue that student affairs educators should shoulder these responsibilities, given their expertise in creating equitable learning environments and addressing issues of oppression, privilege, and power. ACUI is a non-profit educational organization that brings together college union and student activities professionals from hundreds of schools in seven countries.

"A Student Should Have the Privilege of Just Being a Student: Student Activism as Labor," ACUI, July 25, 2019. Reprinted by permission.

As you read, consider the following questions:

1. How do the challenges faced by minority students impact their college experiences?
2. What role should student affairs educators play in addressing the issues faced by student activists, according to this viewpoint?
3. How should institutions respond to the demands of student activists and how can this help alleviate the burdens on these activists?

As student activists with minoritized identities work unpaid to improve their institutions and address institutional oppression, they are met with racial battle fatigue, burnout and exhaustion, and compassion fatigue, all while unable to engage in educationally beneficial college experiences, according to a recent article in *The Review of Higher Education*.

A team of six researchers from five different universities examined the costs minority student activists pay when advocating, unpaid, for institutional change, and they concluded that student affairs educators should be the ones bearing these responsibilities. It's "a job, arguably, student affairs educators should hold," the authors wrote, explaining such professionals have the knowledge and ability to create equitable learning environments for all participants and to address issues of oppression, privilege, and power.

"A Student Should Have the Privilege of Just Being a Student: Student Activism as Labor," illuminates the way minority student activists steer through institutional oppression while interacting with administrators and educators. An examination of the consequences of that activism—academic performance, isolation from peers and family, and physical and emotional exhaustion—then follows.

The six authors comprised two faculty members (Chris Linder, University of Utah; Stephen J. Quaye, Miami University),

What Rights Are Protected in Higher Education?

a women's resource center director (Marvette Lacy, University of Wisconsin–Milwaukee), a visiting assistant professor (Wilson K. Okello, Miami University), and two doctoral students (Ricky E. Roberts, University of Georgia; Alex C. Lange, University of Iowa). Collectively they represent queer white women, black heterosexual men, white queer men, black queer women, multiracial queer men, and black lesbian women. These researchers conducted 30- to 75-minute interviews with 25 students (11 graduate students; 12 undergraduates; two alumni graduated within the year) engaged in identity-based activism, using narrative inquiry to examine how power and privilege had influenced their experiences.

The participants came from 14 different institutions of various size and type. Four of the activists were Asian-American, five black, three multi-racial, 11 white, one Arab, and one Latina. Seventeen were women, three were men, and five were either transgender or gender-queer; 14 identified as straight, four as queer, three as bisexual, two as lesbian, one as pansexual, and one as unknown.

Data were analyzed qualitatively using three-cycle manual coding, a process designed by Johnny Saldana, author of "The Coding Manual for Qualitative Researchers," that involves identification of words or short phrases that capture the essence of language-based data. Each team member coded two transcripts, then the team discussed the initial codes and developed a master code list. Two team members then coded each transcript, notes were compared, and discussion identified any coding discrepancies. Finally, codes were grouped into larger themes.

By naming and paying attention to dominance and oppression in their data, what was interpreted from the coding were themes that recognized minoritized students having campus experiences that were neither equitable, nor inclusive.

"Students described experiences with administrators protecting dominance, backlash from administrators and educators, and ways that institutions benefit from the free labor of student activities," the authors wrote. Specifically:

- Activists saw administrators protecting dominance in three primary ways: financially; through freedom of speech claims; and by aligning themselves with the institution over students.
- Backlash included negative reactions by administrators (e.g., withdrawing interpersonal/institutional capital/support) and a sense of disconnection from faculty, staff, family, and peers (e.g., isolation, lack of understanding).
- Student activists in this study were acutely aware of how institutions benefited from their labor related to improving campus climate. Further, many student activists also noted the additional labor expected of minoritized faculty and staff frequently charged with supporting minoritized student activists.

#BlackLivesMatter, Undocuqueer, DACA, and #MeToo are examples of a resurgence of student activism on college campuses, as students have "worked to hold their institutions accountable for racism, transphobia, Islamophobia, xenophobia, and sexism, to name a few," the authors wrote. But there are costs to doing that work, as one student interviewee, Teresa, pointed out.

"A student should have the privilege of just being a student, and it's really weird how that is a privilege, just being a student, but it obviously is because there are people who cannot only be a student," she said, offering examples of how students with minoritized identities often had little choice but to engage in activism.

The team's work reveals the costs to students engaging in unpaid labor tied to diversity and equity on college campuses, "labor in which white, cisgender, nondisabled, wealthy, and male students do not have to engage."

"When students do not have the luxury of 'just being students,' as described by Teresa, they take on more than their fair share of commitment to improving the community, resulting in them having less time to engage in creative, intellectual, and other endeavors that would benefit their growth and development during and beyond college. They experience backlash and resistance from administrators and significant levels of exhaustion and burnout as a result of their activism," the researchers found.

It's far more complicated than simply compensating activists for the work, the team noted, and they instead offered a series of actions student affairs professionals could take:

- Reflect on why activists are ultimately responsible for improving their campuses.
- Develop support systems for students currently engaged in activism.
- Support activists as they work to heal from oppression and the additional labor it required, including by directing more resources to campus counseling centers.
- Understand the significance of emotional, physical, and mental exhaustion among student activists, and work to alleviate the additional labor required of minoritized students.
- Consider the unique interplay between activists' minoritized identities and their activism, resulting in unpaid emotional, mental, and physical labor.

Most importantly, the authors advised student affairs professionals to change the oppressive structures that require students to engage in activism in the first place, asserting that institutional leaders must respond to activists' demands and stop relying on activists' free labor to improve campus environments.

Reference

Linder, C., Quaye, S.J., Lange, A.C., Roberts, R.E., Lacy, M.C., & Okello, W.K. (2019). "A Student Should Have the Privilege of Just Being a Student": Student Activism as Labor. *The Review of Higher Education, 42*, 37-62.

VIEWPOINT 2

| *"Universities should support freedom of speech, including unpopular ideas, but not without challenging them."*

Four Fundamental Principles for Upholding Freedom of Speech on Campus

Adrienne Stone

In this viewpoint, Adrienne Stone explains how the issue of free speech within universities has gained attention amidst recent on-campus upheavals. Although various university leaders have upheld free speech, it must continue to be not only guarded, but a culture of intellectual autonomy must be created on campus. Such a culture propels knowledge acquisition and nurtures critical discernment. In spite of the occasional necessity of circumscribing free speech, Stone lists four essential principles for advancing free speech on campus. Ultimately, universities need to navigate the terrain of free speech carefully, balancing intellectual freedom and safeguarding the well-being and parity of their diverse academic communities. Adrienne Stone is a professor at Melbourne Law School in Australia and director of the Centre for Comparative Constitutional Studies.

"Four fundamental principles for upholding freedom of speech on campus," by Adrienne Stone, The Conversation, October 14, 2018. https://theconversation.com/four-fundamental-principles-for-upholding-freedom-of-speech-on-campus-104690. Licensed under CC-BY-ND 4.0 International.

As you read, consider the following questions:

1. What are the four fundamental principles that universities should abide by in terms of freedom of speech on campus, according to Stone?
2. How does Stone argue for the importance of tolerating offensive ideas within universities?
3. How should universities balance the protection of free speech with the concerns of students and staff, according to this viewpoint?

It goes without saying—or at least it ought to—that freedom of speech should be a core value of universities. As a scholar of freedom of speech and a university academic, it has been gratifying to see so many Vice Chancellors (and a former Chief Justice of the High Court) take it so seriously.

This attention to freedom of speech is a response to recent controversies about on campus. Bettina Arndt's campus tour met with rowdy and obstructive demonstrations. Students have accused each other of bullying and censorship. And last year, La Trobe University academic Roz Ward was briefly suspended for misconduct for her controversial views on Australia's flag in a Facebook post.

Temperatures are running high enough that universities have occasionally been forced to cancel controversial speakers for fear of the disruption caused by protesters. These controversies are not new. But it's high time for universities to think very carefully about freedom of speech and they should prevent speakers from speaking in only very rare cases.

The Special Context of the University

One thing to consider is there is no context in which freedom of speech constitutes an absolute right to say anything at all. All serious thinkers about freedom of speech and all legal systems —even the US, which has the strongest protection of free speech in the world—recognise some limits on freedom of speech. The difficult question is where those limits properly lie.

It's also important to remember universities have a special responsibility for the attainment of knowledge and for the education of students. These goals require high levels of intellectual freedom, including freedom of speech. Freedom of speech enables researchers and students to discover new things, communicate and test their ideas, and foster and develop critical thinking skills.

But freedom of speech in universities is a means to that end, and not an end in itself.

The Four Fundamental Principles

Because of this responsibility, universities should be guided by four fundamental free speech principles.

1. Unorthodox Ideas Should Be Welcomed and Offensive Ideas Must Be Tolerated

The proper advancement of knowledge and learning requires a high degree of freedom of speech. It's very important orthodoxies can be challenged and ideas subject to debate and criticism. It's through freedom of speech, for example, that women and minorities challenged established ideas about their inferiority.

A university community is necessarily one in which people disagree and will often do so in deep and unchangeable ways. Those disagreements mean sometimes public debate on campus will be highly offensive and upsetting. Even so, offensive ideas must be tolerated.

Our willingness to extend the right to people we disagree with is at the heart of freedom of speech. After all, popular or mainstream ideas generally need no protection. There is no question, for example, that Bettina Arndt should be permitted to speak on university campuses, as should those who oppose her.

2. Protest Is Crucial to the Proper Exercise of Free Speech on Campus and Should Be Permitted and Facilitated

The protection of protest is just as important as protecting the expression of unorthodox and unpopular ideas. Protest—whether by environmentalists or anti-abortion activists—is an important means for the expression of unorthodox and unpopular ideas, as

> ### EXAMPLES OF STUDENT ACTIVISM
>
> Throughout history, students have protested against many social issues, ranging from education to the environment. Here are five examples of student activism.
>
> #### School Strike for Climate
>
> On Friday 20th September 2019, approximately four million people—mostly students—gathered across the world for the Global Climate Strike, part of the School Strike for Climate movement. In the UK, an estimated 300,000 people took part in the protests.
>
> The protests were inspired by Swedish student Greta Thunberg, who boycotted school every Friday to demand that the government fight climate change. The Global Climate Strike demonstrated how passionately students cared about climate change and helped spread more awareness about the urgent action needed to tackle it.
>
> #### Fossil Free Stanford
>
> Another example of student activism in response to climate change is the Fossil Free Stanford campaign, led by students at Stanford University. Fossil Free Stanford demanded that the university withdraw its investments in fossil fuel companies.
>
> In 2014, Stanford University announced that it would no longer invest in coal extraction companies, a victory for the campaign and the fight against climate change.
>
> #### Highgate School
>
> Female students at Highgate School in the UK recently led walkouts to protest the school's handling of sexual assault allegations and the

well as for a response to them. We should expect protest to be part of university life and universities should both permit and facilitate them.

Obviously, universities will be in the middle of fierce disputes between opposing elements of the community and working out a balance of interests will be difficult. If there are loud and chaotic protests that require significant security, it will also be expensive.

> prevailing misogynistic attitudes among male students. The protests came after the school was deemed to have poorly handled over 200 allegations of sexual assault.
>
> Highgate School announced that a review into the allegations would be carried out and take necessary actions.
>
> ### March for Our Lives
>
> In March 2018, approximately one million students took part in March for Our Lives, a USA-wide demonstration calling for stricter gun control laws after a school shooting in Florida. Students gave speeches about how gun violence had impacted their lives, while protesters demanded more thorough background checks for gun sales. March for Our Lives was one of the biggest protests in the history of the USA, unequivocally demonstrating that younger generations want change.
>
> ### 2020 A-Level Results Protests
>
> In 2020, A-Level students across the UK protested against the algorithm used by the government to determine A-Level results following the cancellation of exams due to the Covid-19 pandemic. The government's flawed algorithm led to over 280,000 results unfairly downgraded. Downgraded exam results meant students lost places on university courses and apprenticeship schemes, which they had applied to using their predicted grades.
>
> The widespread criticism of the algorithm forced the government to adjust their policy and award A-Level results based on students' predicted grades.
>
> "Five of the best examples of student activism," by Aimee Clyne, Student Hut, April 30, 2021.

But it's not fair to place the cost of security entirely on those provoking the protest (giving protesters an effective heckler's veto). Nor is it fair to place it on those protesting (given the importance of protest as a mechanism for free speech).

If governments are serious about protecting freedom of speech on campus they should fund universities in a way that makes it possible for them to balance free speech and protest on their campuses. A free speech fund for each university seems like a small price to pay for something so fundamental.

3. The University Must Protect the Pursuit of Knowledge

Because universities have a responsibility to promote the attainment of knowledge and education, they also need to protect those activities from people who blatantly disregard evidence, research and scholarly standards of inquiry.

Universities should not be required to give a platform to those who peddle nonsense—especially dangerous nonsense. Universities are quite within their rights to deny anti-vaxxers, Holocaust deniers, flat earthers and others from the use of their facilities.

The line between the unorthodox and nonsense can, of course, be blurry and universities should be very careful about how they exercise this power. They might choose instead to permit such speakers but to ensure a platform for their critics that's at least as prominent.

Free speech scholar and Columbia University President Lee Bollinger provided a good example of this kind of action when he permitted the appearance of then President of Iran, Mahmoud Ahmadinejad, on Columbia's campus but personally introduced him with a series of sharp challenges. Universities should support freedom of speech, including unpopular ideas, but not without challenging them.

4. The University's Intellectual Climate Must Be Inclusive

Universities can't be sure they have the best researchers and students unless everyone has an equal opportunity to attend and participate in university life. For this reason, universities need to take seriously the concerns of students and staff who are affected by the exercise of the free speech rights of others.

Students who claim controversial ideas threaten their safety have been widely condemned. Hurt feelings themselves provide no good reason to take action against speech or speakers. But these students are often arguing that ideas perpetuated by these speakers are a barrier to their equality and can lead to discrimination or violence.

At least in public forums on campus, a university should very rarely prevent speakers from spreading their message. But students concerned about their equality and safety on campus should not be ignored or ridiculed.

Universities need to engage with their students about their concerns, take steps to protect their physical safety and well-being, and ensure these students can respond on their own behalf. In serious cases, where students are subject to unfair and abusive commentary, the university ought to use its own powers of speech to defend them publicly.

VIEWPOINT 3

> "Universal autonomy is upheld as a bulwark for academic freedom, which may be circumscribed to protect the rights and freedoms of others."

Academic Freedom as a Source of Rights' Violations

Monika Stachowiak-Kudla

In this excerpted viewpoint, Monika Stachowiak-Kudła argues that while academic freedom is a concept that can be interpreted in many ways, common legal ground can be found in certain aspects of this issue. A 1997 recommendation in Europe—which was globally endorsed—defines academic freedom as the unencumbered right to teach and disseminate knowledge. Courts generally concur that academic freedom comes with safeguards from unwarranted interference and shields academics. Relatedly, the concept of universal autonomy is accepted as crucial for academic freedom. Yet the strength of academic freedom is affected when it clashes with other rights or autonomy. In courts, proportionality analysis plays a role, with courts favoring limitations for the protection of human rights. Despite the lack of a universal definition of academic freedom, courts have been tasked to resolve conflicts involving academic freedom, but in a limited manner as conflicts rarely lead to courtroom disputes.

"Academic freedom as a source of rights' violations: a European perspective," by Monika Stachowiak-Kudła, Springer Nature, May 8, 2021. https://link.springer.com/article/10.1007/s10734-021-00718-3. Licensed under CC-BY 4.0 International.

What Rights Are Protected in Higher Education?

Monika Stachowiak-Kudła is an assistant professor of law at Siedlce University in Poland.

As you read, consider the following questions:

1. What key aspects of academic freedom are highlighted in this viewpoint?
2. How do the above aspects of academic freedom relate to the concept of universal autonomy?
3. Why do conflicts of principles, including academic freedom, rarely lead to courtroom disputes?

The application of academic freedom may lead to a violation of individual rights, such as the right to respect private life or institutional rights such as university autonomy, or the right of the religious community to self-determination. These collisions between rights are resolved by constitutional courts either according to the proportionality test or by balancing the rights. This paper investigates cases from Czechia, Germany, Italy, Poland, and Spain, where academic freedom collided with other constitutional rights, in order to determine methods for resolving these types of conflicts. This analysis demonstrates the way in which proportionality allows the construction of the content of academic freedom. It also shows the reasons why academic freedom could become a weak right and why sometimes it is a strong right.

Introduction

Academic freedom has many definitions and is understood differently (Altbach 2001). In the 1997 Recommendation Concerning the Status of Higher-Education Teaching Personnel, signed by all countries included in this study, academic freedom is equated with "the right, without constriction by prescribed doctrine, to freedom of teaching and discussion, freedom in carrying out research and disseminating and publishing the results thereof, freedom to express freely their opinion about the institution or system in which they work, freedom from institutional censorship and freedom to participate in professional or representative academic bodies" (UNESCO, 11 November 1997). Moreover, some lawyers link the protection of intellectual property with the development of academic freedom (e.g., Davies 2015, 991). Academic freedom is a defensive right, and therefore one that protects scientific and teaching activities against the interference of the state and other authorities, including university and faculty authorities. This important aspect of academic freedom is often taken up in the literature (Enders et al. 2013, 23) particularly in the context of knowledge creation (Karran 2009b, 191; Rittberger and Richardson 2019, 324; Beiter et al., 2016, 272). Academic freedom serves to identify the truth. It is also seen as an act "in the best interests of others, the future of others and other futures" (Gibbs 2016, 184, see also Rena and Li 2013, 511; Thorens 2006, 87–110).

According to Alexy's theory (2000, 2002), fundamental rights and freedoms, which also include academic freedom, are also principles and may collide with other rights. The application of academic freedom may lead to a violation of other individual or institutional rights. The collision between two or more rights is settled by constitutional courts and international tribunals by applying the principle of proportionality (Rivers 2014, 413; Jackson 2015, 3094–3196; Brems and Lavrysen 2015). In the traditional approach, the principle of proportionality is used to determine whether a statutory limitation imposed on a fundamental right is justifiable (Feteris 2008).

In recent literature, there is a growing interest in the merits and detriments of the principle of proportionality (Ramshaw 2019; Stacey 2019; Alexy 2020; Poscher 2020). The application of proportionality in the area of academic freedom is a less discussed issue, yet of vital importance to the ongoing debate for two reasons. Firstly, academic freedom can collide not only with other individual rights but also with institutional rights. This aspect has not been sufficiently analyzed in literature. Secondly, in some countries (France, Hungary, Italy, Poland, and Spain), academic freedom does not have a legal definition and in the event of a dispute, courts have to determine the essence of this right. Proportionality promotes a dialog between the judge and lawmaker thereby making the content of academic freedom concrete. The main advantage of proportionality is the help it offers in defining the minimum core content of academic freedom.

This paper strives to clarify how academic freedom is understood in the jurisprudence of constitutional courts.

[…]

Concluding Remarks

Some elements of academic freedom are understood similarly by the courts. First, academic freedom protects the individual from unjustified interference from public authority and/or university. Menand (1996) also points out that academic freedom protects academics from other academics. Second, university autonomy exists to protect academic freedom. Third, academic freedom may be limited in order to protect rights and freedoms of other people.

The freedom of scientific research in the assessment of constitutional courts is primarily freedom to choose subjects for research, choose their methodology, and publish their results. The three aspects of the freedom of scientific research are also indicated in the literature (see also: Feldman 1989, 507). Independence in the selection of didactic content and the used methods as well as the right to express scientific opinions are important aspects of the freedom of teaching in the assessment of constitutional courts.

The investigated cases prove that academic freedom can conflict with the individual rights, such as the right to respect private life, with institutional rights such as university autonomy, or the right of the religious community to self-determination. In collision with the right to respect private life and the right of the religious community to self-determination, it turns out to be a weak right. Obviously it does not mean that in the conflict with other fundamental rights not considered in this article, it could not turn out to be a strong right. Answering this question requires extending the research to other jurisdictions and analyzing subsequent conflicts of principles. Academic freedom is a strong right when it collides with the university's right to autonomy, which results mainly from the fact that the main purpose of the university's autonomy is the protection of academic freedom. Of course, one can argue whether the analysis of only five decisions of the courts is sufficient to state with certainty that a given fundamental right is weak, that is, it loses in the collision with other rights. However, the courts of all countries examined here adjudicate in a system with a doctrine of *jurisprudence constante*. In such a system, a line of authority emerges, the essence of which is that most courts dealing with a similar case decide it identically or similarly. Therefore, it can be expected with high probability for another collision of academic freedom with a given right, the court will rule consistently with previous verdicts.

My research also revealed that, when the courts decide the conflict between academic freedom and university autonomy, the latter is perceived as a distinct right but not another aspect of academic freedom.

Academic freedom is exposed to a proportionality analysis because the constitutional courts clearly prefer the limitation clause based on the protection of other individual rights. However, elements of the proportionality test were clearly identified only in three examined cases: German, Italian, and Polish. In these judgments, three criteria were decisive: the existence of a legitimate aim; the adoption of a less restrictive means test; and the use of a balancing exercise, or strict proportionality. The Italian, Polish, and Spanish cases prove that the lack of a legal definition or consent about the essence of academic freedom does not prevent the court from resolving a conflict.

Finally, the research indicates that the conflicts of principles, one of which is academic freedom, rarely take the form of a dispute in court. Consequently, there are not many cases which could be used by judges and scientists.

References

Alexy, R. (2000). On the structure of legal principles. *Ratio Juris, 13*(3), 294–304.

Alexy, R. (2002). *A theory of constitutional rights,* Oxford University Press.

Alexy, R. (2020). Non-positivistic concept of constitutional rights. *International Journal for the Semiotics of Law, 33,* 35–46.

Altbach, F. (2001). Academic freedom: International realities and challenges. *Higher Education, 41,* 205–219.

Beiter, K. D., Karran, T., & Appiagyei-Atua, K. (2016). Academic freedom and its protection in the law of European States: Measuring an international human right. *European Journal of Comparative Law and Governance, 3*(3), 254–345.

Brems, E., & Lavrysen, L. (2015). Don't use a sledgehammer to crack a nut: Less restrictive means in the case law of the European Court of Human Rights. *Human Rights Law Review, 15*(1), 139–168.

Davies, M. (2015). Academic freedom: A lawyer's perspective. *Higher Education, 70,* 987–1002.

Feldman, D. (1989). The nature of legal scholarship. *Modern Law Review, 52*(4), 498–517.

Feteris, E. T. (2008). The rational reconstruction of weighing and balancing on the basis of teleological-evaluative considerations in the justification of judicial decisions. *Ratio Juris, 21*(4), 481–495.

Gibbs, A. (2016). Academic freedom in international higher education: Right or responsibility? *Ethics and Education, 11*(2), 175–185.

Karran, T. (2009b). Academic freedom in Europe: Reviewing Unesco's recommendation. *British Journal of Educational Studies, 57*(2), 191–215.

Poscher, R. (2020). Resuscitation of a phantom? On Robert Alexy's latest attempt to save his concept of principle. *Ratio Juris, 33*(2), 134–149.

Rena, K., & Li, J. (2013). Academic freedom and university autonomy: A higher education policy perspective. *Higher Education Policy, 26*(4), 507–522.

Rittberger, B., & Richardson, J. (2019). What happens when we do not defend academic freedom. *Journal of European Public Policy, 26*(3), 324.

Thorens, J. (2006). Liberties, freedom and autonomy: A few reflections on academia's estate. *Higher Education Policy, 19*(1), 87–110.

Stacey, R. (2019). The magnetism of moral reasoning and the principle of proportionality in comparative constitutional adjudication. *The American Journal of Comparative Law, 67*(2), 435–475.

Thorens, J. (2006). Liberties, freedom and autonomy: A few reflections on academia's estate. *Higher Education Policy, 19*(1), 87–110.

Viewpoint 4

> *"In a climate where relations between academia and industry are encouraged and industry funding for research continues to grow, academics must guard against threats to academic freedom posed by industry support."*

Academic Research Funded by Big Companies Is Compromised

Lisa Bero

In this viewpoint, Lisa Bero explains how over the last two decades industry funding of global medical research has risen significantly while government and non-profit support has fallen. In fact, industry support already exceeded public support by 2011. This trend is not limited to medicine, with various other sectors (including food, chemicals, mining, technology, and automobiles) investing in research endeavors, thus posing a threat to academic freedom. Many research contracts include clauses granting industry funders the power to veto research publication, and many scholars face industry efforts to suppress unfavorable findings, for example pharmaceutical companies' historical attempts to bury research questioning their products. Institutional oversight remains inadequate, and industry sponsors have been shown to manipulate research, selectively

"When big companies fund academic research, the truth often comes last," by Lisa Bero, The Conversation, October 2, 2019. https://theconversation.com/when-big-companies-fund-academic-research-the-truth-often-comes-last-119164. Licensed under CC BY-ND 4.0 International.

publishing favorable results while suppressing adverse ones. To protect academic freedom, industry funding must come without publication restrictions and governments should prioritize unbiased research. Lisa Bero is a chair and professor of medicines use and health outcomes at the University of Sydney in Australia.

As you read, consider the following questions:

1. How has the major shift in the funding landscape for medical research over the past two decades affected the field of academics?
2. How do industry sponsors often exert control over research findings? Give one example from the viewpoint where industry funding influenced the design and publication of research findings to suit industry interests.
3. According to Bero, how can academic freedom be protected?

Over the last two decades, industry funding for medical research has increased globally, while government and non-profit funding has decreased. By 2011, industry funding, compared to public sources, accounted for two-thirds of medical research worldwide.

Research funding from other industries is increasing too, including food and beverage, chemical, mining, computer and automobile companies. And as a result, academic freedom suffers.

Industry Sponsors Suppress Publication

An early career academic recently sought my advice about her industry-funded research. Under the funding contract—that was signed by her supervisor—she wouldn't be able to publish the results of her clinical trial.

Another researcher, a doctoral student, asked for help with her dissertation. Her work falls under the scope of her PhD supervisor's research funding agreement with a company. This agreement prevented the publication of any work deemed commercial-in-confidence by the industry funder. So, she will not be allowed to submit the papers to fulfil her dissertation requirements.

I come across such stories often and they all have one thing in common. The blocked publications present the sponsoring companies' products in an unfavourable way. While the right to publish is a mainstay of academic freedom, research contracts often include clauses that give the funder the final say on whether the research can be published.

Early career researchers are particularly vulnerable to publication restrictions when companies fund their research. Scientific publication is vital to their career advancement, but their supervisors may control the research group's relationship with industry.

Senior researchers can also be vulnerable to industry suppressing their research. In the 1980s, a pharmaceutical company funded a researcher to compare their brand's thyroid drug to its generic counterparts. The researcher found the generics were as good as the branded products.

The funder then went to great lengths to suppress the publication of her findings, including taking legal action against her and her university.

And there is little institutional oversight. A 2018 study found that, among 127 academic institutions in the United States, only one-third required their faculty to submit research consulting agreements for review by the institution.

And 35% of academic institutions did not think it was necessary for the institution to review such agreements. When consulting agreements were reviewed, only 23% of academic institutions looked at publication rights. And only 19% looked for inappropriate confidentiality provisions, such as prohibiting communication about any aspect of the funded work.

Industry Sponsors Manipulate Evidence

The definition of academic freedom boils down to freedom of inquiry, investigation, research, expression and publication (or dissemination).

Internal industry documents obtained through litigation have revealed many examples of industry sponsors influencing the design and conduct of research, as well as the partial publication of research where only findings favourable to the funder were published.

For instance, in 1981 an influential Japanese study showed an association between passive smoking and lung cancer. It concluded wives of heavy smokers had up to twice the risk of developing lung cancer as wives of non-smokers and that the risk was dose related.

Tobacco companies then funded academic researchers to create a study that would refute these findings. The tobacco companies were involved in every step of the funded work, but kept the extent of their involvement hidden for decades. They framed the research questions, designed the study, collected and provided data, and wrote the final publication.

This publication was used as "evidence" that tobacco smoke is not harmful. It concluded there was no direct evidence passive smoke exposure increased risk of lung cancer. The tobacco industry cited the study in government and regulatory documents to refute the independent data on the harms of passive smoking.

Industry Sponsors Influence Research Agendas

The biggest threat to academic freedom may be the influence industry funders have on the very first stage in the research process: establishing research agendas. This means industry sponsors get unprecedented control over the research questions that get studied.

We recently reviewed research studies that looked at corporate influence on the research agenda. We found industry funding drives researchers to study questions that aim to maximise benefits and minimise harms of their products, distract from independent research that is unfavourable, decrease regulation of their products, and support their legal and policy positions.

In another tobacco-related example, three tobacco companies created and funded The Center for Indoor Air Research that would conduct research to "distract" from evidence for the harms of second-hand smoke. Throughout the 1990s, this centre funded dozens of research projects that suggested components of indoor air, such as carpet off-gases or dirty air filters, were more harmful than tobacco.

The sugar industry also attempted to shift the focus away from evidence showing an association between sugar and heart disease. It was only recently revealed that, in the 1960s, the sugar industry paid scientists at Harvard University to minimise the link between sugar and heart disease, and to shift the blame from sugar to fat as being responsible for the heart disease epidemic.

The paper's authors suggested many of today's dietary recommendations may have been largely shaped by the sugar industry. And some experts have since questioned whether such misinformation can have led to today's obesity crisis.

Coca-Cola and Mars have also funded university research on physical activity to divert attention away from the association of their products with obesity.

How Do We Protect Academic Freedom?

In a climate where relations between academia and industry are encouraged and industry funding for research continues to grow, academics must guard against threats to academic freedom posed by industry support.

Academic freedom means industry funding must come with no strings attached. Researchers must ask themselves if accepting industry funding contributes to the mission of discovering new knowledge or to an industry research agenda aimed at increasing profits.

Governments or independent consortia of multiple funders, including government and industry, must ensure support for research that meets the needs of the public.

When research is supported by industry, funders should not dictate the design, conduct or publication of the research. Many universities have and enforce policies that prevent such restrictions, but this is not universal. Open science, including publication of protocols and data, can expose industry interference in research.

Scientists should never sign, or let their institution sign, an agreement that gives a funder power to prevent dissemination of their research findings. Universities and scientific journals must protect emerging researchers and support all academics in fending off industry influence and preserving academic freedom.

Periodical and Internet Sources Bibliography

The following articles have been selected to supplement the diverse views presented in this chapter.

Jennifer Berkshire, "Why Teachers Are Dropping Out," the *Nation,* February 21, 2021. https://www.thenation.com/article/society/teachers-covid-culture-wars/.

Editorial Board, "These Universities Are Pushing Back on Censorious Students Finally," *Washington Post,* April 29, 2023. https://www.washingtonpost.com/opinions/2023/04/29/university-campus-free-speech-censorship-fight/.

Colleen Flaherty, "Calling It Quits," *Inside Higher Education*, July 2022. https://www.insidehighered.com/news/2022/07/05/professors-are-leaving-academe-during-great-resignation#at_pco=cfd-1.0.

Nicholas Francis Havey, Demeturie Toso-Lafaele Gogue, and Mitchell J. Chang, "Tracing Institutional Change: How Student Activism Concerning Diversity Facilitates Administrative Action," *Journal of Diversity in Higher Education, 2022.* https://doi.org/10.1037/dhe0000446.

Doug McAdam, Priya Fielding-Singh, Krystal Laryea, and Jennifer Hill, "Predicting the Onset, Evolution, And Postgraduate Impact of College Activism," *Mobilization: An International Quarterly*, July 11, 2022. https://doi.org/10.17813/1086-671X-27-2-125.

Michele O'Dwyer, Raffaele Filieri, and Lisa O'Malley, "Establishing Successful University–Industry Collaborations: Barriers and Enablers Deconstructed," *Journal of Technology Transfer*, 2023. https://doi.org/10.1007/s10961-022-09932-2.

Cristina Bianca Pocol, Liana Stanca, Dan-Cristian Dabiha, Iona Delia Pop, and Segiu Miscoiu, "Knowledge Co-Creation and Sustainable Education in the Labor Market-Driven University–Business Environment," *Frontiers in Environmental Science*, February 18, 2022. https://doi.org/10.3389/fenvs.2022.781075.

Stephen John Quaye, Chris Linder, Terah J. Stewart, and Erin M. Satterwhite, "A Review of Scholarship on College Student Activism From 2000 to 2020," *Higher Education: Handbook of*

Theory and Research. February 23, 2022. https://link.springer.com/referenceworkentry/10.1007/978-3-030-76660-3_5.

Amia Srinivasan, "Cancelled: Can I Speak Freely?" *London Review of Books*, June 29, 2023. https://www.lrb.co.uk/the-paper/v45/n13/amia-srinivasan/cancelled.

Megan Zahneis and Audrey Williams June, "In These Red States, Professors Are Eyeing the Exits," *Chronicle of Higher Education*, September 7, 2023. https://www.chronicle.com/article/in-these-red-states-professors-are-eyeing-the-exits?utm_source=Iterable&utm_medium=email&utm_campaign=campaign_7671654_nl_Academe-Today_date_20230908&cid=at.

For Further Discussion

Chapter 1
1. According to the viewpoints in this chapter, what challenges do students face in making the decision to pursue college or university degrees? Will these challenges differ for first generation, returning adult, and minority students?
2. Based on what you read in the viewpoints in this chapter, do you think the potential benefits of a college degree are convincing enough to persuade more people to attend college? Why or why not?
3. How would you design a new college curriculum that effectively reflects the purpose of higher education today, including preparing students for the workforce while also helping them grow personally and intellectually?

Chapter 2
1. According to the viewpoints in this chapter, what factors should be considered when evaluating choices for post-secondary education in the U.S.?
2. Based on what you read in the viewpoints in this chapter, what are the advantages and disadvantages of alternatives to four-year institutions of higher education, such as community colleges, certificates, and stackable credentials?
3. In the context of higher education in the U.S., what are the key differences between for-profit and non-profit colleges, and how do these differences influence the educational experiences and outcomes for students?

Chapter 3
1. According to the viewpoints in this chapter, how do you think colleges and universities can balance protecting freedom of speech and addressing (potentially) offensive

speech and hate speech? What role could student activism play in achieving this balance?
2. Based on what you read in the viewpoints in this chapter, how does the controversy around discussions of race in higher education highlight the challenges faced by students and professors?
3. How might the increasing interest by students in political and civic engagement influence the broader social, political, and cultural landscape of the United States?

Chapter 4

1. According to the viewpoints in this chapter, how can politics affect the overall climate and culture of higher education institutions for students and faculty?
2. Based on what you read in the viewpoints in this chapter, what potential challenges and tensions can universities face in balancing concerns of free speech and safety and equality on campuses?
3. According to the viewpoints in this chapter, how do the increasing influences of industry funding of academic research impact the integrity of research in general and universities in particular?

Organizations to Contact

The editors have compiled the following list of organizations concerned with the issues debated in this book. The descriptions are derived from materials provided by the organizations. All have publications or information available for interested readers. The list was compiled on the date of publication of the present volume; the information provided here may change. Be aware that many organizations take several weeks or longer to respond to inquiries, so allow as much time as possible.

Association for Career and Technical Education (ACTE)

1410 King St.
Alexandria, VA 22314
(800) 826-9972
email: acte@acteonline.org
website: www.acteonline.org

The Association for Career and Technical Education is a national education association dedicated to the advancement of education that prepares youth and adults for successful careers. The ACTE prepares secondary, post-secondary, and adult students with technical, academic, and employable skills for success in the workplace and in further education.

Coalition for College

P.O. Box 850
Colchester, VT 05446
email: info@coalitionforcollege.org
website: www.coalitionforcollegeaccess.org

Founded in 2015, the Coalition for College is an association of member schools that have committed to supporting lower-income, under-resourced, and first-generation college students with financial aid programs and other support resources. The website offers information to assist students and families from historically underrepresented groups as they navigate the college application process and during their enrollment. For example, the "MyCoalition" feature offers a set of college-planning tools to help students stay organized as they research and apply to schools.

College Board
250 Vesey Street
New York, NY 10281
United States
(866) 630-9305
website: www.collegeboard.org

Founded in 1900, the College Board is a non-profit organization dedicated to expanding access to higher education in the United States. The membership association includes over six thousand colleges and universities, and its resources are utilized by more than seven million college applicants every year. The website includes information on various programs designed to encourage college readiness and success.

Federal Student Aid
1 (800) 433-3243
website: https://studentaid.gov

Sponsored by the U.S. Department of Education, the office of Federal Student Aid provides grants, loans, and work-study funds for college or career school. Its website provides information on the types of financial aid available from the government and other sources, and includes instructions on filling out the FAFSA. The office annually provides more than $120 billion in financial aid to help pay for college or career school.

Foundation for Individual Rights and Expression (FIRE)

510 Walnut St. Suite 1250
Philadelphia, PA 19106
(215) 717-3473
email: fire@thefire.org
website: www.thefire.org

FIRE is a non-profit civil liberties group that protects free speech and academic freedom on college campuses. It educates students and educators about their rights and has offered legal support to those whose rights have been challenged.

Jobs for the Future (JFF)

(617) 728-4446
website: www.jff.org

Jobs for the Future (JFF) helps lifelong learners get the education they need to advance on the job. Particular focus areas include skills training, workforce development, and literacy. JFF drives transformation of the American workforce and education systems to achieve equitable economic advancement for all.

The Project on Student Debt

1300 Clay Street, Suite 1020
Oakland, CA 94612
(510) 318-7900
website: https://ticas.org/our-work/student-debt

The Project on Student Debt works to identify cost-effective student loan solutions. The Project is an initiative of the Institute for College Access & Success, a non-profit independent research and policy organization dedicated to making college more available and affordable to people of all backgrounds.

U.S. Department of Education
400 Maryland Avenue, SW
Washington, DC 20202
1 (800) 872-5327
website: www.ed.gov

The U.S. Department of Education oversees education at all levels. Its website explains why you should go to college and how to pay for it. It also gives useful information on available loans, making loan payments, and loan defaults.

Bibliography of Books

Sonja Ardoin and Becky Martinez. *Straddling Class in the Academy: 26 Stories of Students, Administrators, and Faculty from Poor and Working Class Backgrounds and Their Compelling Lessons for Higher Education Policy and Practice.* Sterling, VA: Stylus, 2019.

Michael N. Bastedo, Philip G. Altbach, and Patricia J. Gumport. *American Higher Education in the Twenty-First Century: Social, Political and Economic Challenges.* 5th ed. Baltimore, MD: Johns Hopkins University Press, 2023.

Amy J. Binder and Jeffrey L. Kidder. *The Channels of Student Activism: How the Left and Right are Winning (and Losing) in Campus Politics Today.* Chicago, IL: University of Chicago Press, 2021.

Michael M. Crow and William B. Dabars. *The Fifth Wave: The Evolution of American Higher Education.* Baltimore, MD: Johns Hopkins University Press, 2023.

Donald A. Downs. *Free Speech and Liberal Education.* Washington, DC: Cato Institute, 2020.

Sean R. Gallagher. *The Future of University Credentials: New Developments at the Intersection of Higher Education and Hiring.* Cambridge, MA: Harvard University Press, 2023.

Sara Goldrick-Rab. *Paying the Price: College Costs, Financial Aid, and the Betrayal of the American Dream.* Chicago, IL: University of Chicago Press, 2017.

Guilbert C. Hentschke, Vicente M. Lechuga, and William G. Tierney, eds. *For-Profit Colleges and Universities: Their Markets, Regulation, Performance.* New York, NY: Routledge, 2023.

Andrew J. Hoffman. *Expanding the Impact of Academic Research in Today's World.* Standford, CA: Stanford University Press, 2021.

Michael B. Horn and Bob Moesta. *Choosing College: How to Make Better Learning Decisions Throughout Your Life*. Ashland, OR: Tantor and Blackstone.

Joshua Kim and Edward J. Maloney. *Learning Innovation and the Future of Higher Education*. Baltimore, MD: Johns Hopkins University Press, 2020.

John S. Levin and Susan T. Kater, eds. *Understanding Community Colleges*. New York, NY: Routledge, 2018.

Josh Mitchell. *The Debt Trap: How Student Loans Became a National Catastrophe*. New York, NY: Simon & Schuster, 2022.

Jerusha Osberg Conner. *The New Student Activists: The Rise of Neoactivism on College Campuses*. Baltimore, MD: Johns Hopkins University Press, 2020.

Henry Reichman. *Understanding Academic Freedom*. Baltimore, MD: Johns Hopkins University Press, 2021.

John R. Thelin, *A History of American Higher Education*, 3rd ed. Baltimore, MD: Johns Hopkins University Press, 2019.

Michelle Van Noy and Paul L. Gaston. *Credentials: Understanding the Problems. Identifying the Opportunities. Create the Solutions*. New York, NY: Routledge 2022.

Index

A

academic freedom, 14, 94–95, 150–155, 157–162
activism, 14, 18, 125, 135–136, 138-141, 163, 166
   Black Lives Matter, 135
   climate change, 146
   gun control, 147
   #MeToo, 135, 140
   sexual assault, 146–147
associate degree, 25, 28, 30–31, 66, 84

B

baby boomers, 46
bachelor's (four-year) 16, 23–25, 28–32, 37, 45, 51, 62, 65–66, 80–82, 84
Biden, Jill, 65
Biden Administration, 21, 43–44
business, 84, 87, 91, 102–104, 163

C

certification (certificate) programs, 25, 30, 31, 82–84
citizenship, 15, 100–101, 106, 118–122, 125
   voting, 118, 121, 131
communities, 45, 64–67, 75, 103, 109, 113, 124, 130–131, 133 143
   university communities, 124, 126
   web communities, 89
community college, 29, 62, 64–76, 89, 96, 103, 165, 172
costs,
   "free college," 26–27
   return on investment (ROI), 14, 22, 45
   room and board, 34, 48–49
   tuition, 16–17, 21, 26–27, 33–34, 39, 45, 48–49, 67, 91–92
counselors, 49, 53, 55, 68
COVID-19 pandemic, 17, 21–22, 33, 38–40, 65, 67, 85, 147
"credentials gap," 24, 31
critical race theory (CRT), 107–109, 114, 116–117, 107
   See also teaching
critical thinking, 13, 15, 99, 102, 105, 122, 145
curriculum (curricula), 14, 55, 72, 76, 94–95, 99, 102–103, 105, 124, 130–131, 165

D

democracy,
   in Europe, 123–124
   in the United States, 99–100, 106
demographics, 15, 21, 23, 100
diploma,
   college, 24
   high school, 25, 30–31, 45
disabilities (disability), 35–37, 44

distance learning (education), 38, 86–88, 93, 96
diversity, equity, and inclusion (DEI), 99, 107–110, 113, 129–132

E

economists, 12, 16
employers, 31, 63, 66, 81–82, 90, 95, 102, 104–106, 133
enrollment, 15, 22, 33–35, 38, 59, 81, 168
   community college, 65, 67
   online classes, 89

F

faculty:
   and academic freedom, 152
   and academic knowledge, 136
   and activism, 135, 138, 140
   and diversity, equity, and inclusion (DEI) programs, 129–131
   and feedback, 73–76,
   and for-profit (proprietary) schools, 86
   and humanities, 105
   and online education, 86, 93–94
   and politics, 166
   laying off, 39
   representation, 110, 112–113
   research projects, 67, 159
   rights, 14, 17
   finances, 46, 50

financial aid, 34, 48, 50–51, 53, 168, 171
financial planning, 48–50, 52–54
first generation, 54, 165
for-profit (proprietary) universities, 62–63, 85–86, 88–91, 93–97, 165, 171
free speech, 14, 18, 135–136, 143–146, 148–149, 166, 171

G

government, 11, 15–16, 35, 44, 131, 146–147, 157, 158, 160–161
graduation, 15, 47, 51–52, 129, 131
   graduation rates, 62, 81, 110

H

health, 11, 45, 87, 118–119, 158
high school diploma, 31
   See under diploma
high school students, 33, 35, 51, 89, 111
humanities, 101–105

J

job market, 16, 24, 90

M

men, 21, 36, 51, 139
military, 11, 37, 91–93
millennials, 46
minority students, 21, 71, 145, 165
   African American, 35

Asian American, 51, 130, 132, 139
Black, 30, 71, 110, 115, 122, 130, 132, 139
Hispanic, 71
Indigenous, 130, 132
Latino/a (Latinx), 30, 35, 50, 139
Mexican, 51
students of color, 70–71, 75, 130–132

N

Nigeria, 38
non-profit schools, 62–63, 85–86, 88–89, 90–91, 165
nursing, 65, 83–84

O

online courses,
 See under technology
Organization for Economic Cooperation and Development (OECD), 36

P

parents, 14, 30, 49, 54–56, 63, 86, 92–93, 115
personal growth, 14, 22, 25
politicians, 12, 14, 114, 135
politics, 21, 107–109, 116–117, 121, 131, 166, 171
postgraduate (professional) degrees, 25, 28–29, 163
poverty, 11, 35

presidents of higher education institutions, 38–39
principle of proportionality, 150–154
private colleges and universities, 16, 34, 39, 48–49, 93, 120
public colleges and universities, 16, 48–49

R

retention, 51–52, 81, 84, 110

S

scholarships, 16, 49–50, 54, 56, 74
social cognitive career theory (SCCT), 50
speakers on campus, 135, 144, 148–149
stackable programs, 81
STEM, 101, 104–105, 111
student affairs educators, 137–138, 141
student loan debt, 14, 16, 21, 22, 44, 62, 96
 and home ownership, 43, 46
 and net worth, 46–47
 and small business formation, 45, 47
 cancellation, 44
Syria, 38

T

teaching, 25, 67, 74–75, 77, 90, 93–94, 152–153

critical race theory (CRT), 107–109, 114–117
Recommendation Concerning the Status of Higher-Education Teaching Personnel, 151
technology, 50, 84, 87–88, 93, 100, 102, 104, 157, 163
  digital divides, 21
  online courses, 17, 84, 94

U

Uganda, 38
unemployment, 24, 45

V

veterans, 91–92

W

women:
  and access to education, 21, 36, 38
  and bachelor's degree completion rate, 51
  and freedom of speech, 145
  and student loan debt, 47
  minority women, 50, 139
  women's rights, 11, 135

Y

Yemen, 37